"Heaven is a surprisingly popular topic in our culture—there is no shortage of books, films, and other media exploring the afterlife. But what does the Bible say? God has provided us with a tantalizing glimpse of Heaven in His Word. Chip Ingram helps us navigate Scripture's teaching and separate fact from fiction in this practical, readable book."

—**Jim Daly**, president, Focus on the Family

"My friend Chip Ingram is a compelling communicator of Truth. *The Real Heaven* shows us why Heaven matters and gives us guidance as we live with an eternal perspective and personal hope. Don't miss this book!"

—**Jack Graham**, pastor, Prestonwood Baptist Church

"Understanding Heaven is not a waste of time. For Christians, it's one of the most important things we can do! Hope in the promise of what God has prepared for us in the future can make the present much more meaningful, and Chip helps us cling to that hope as he explains *The Real Heaven*."

—**Dave Stone**, pastor, Southeast Christian Church, Louisville, KY

THE
REAL
HEAVEN

Books by Chip Ingram

Good to Great in God's Eyes
God: As He Longs for You to See Him
Love, Sex, and Lasting Relationships
Finding God When You Need Him Most
Overcoming Emotions That Destroy (with Becca Johnson)
Culture Shock
True Spirituality
The Invisible War
The Real Heaven

THE REAL HEAVEN

What the Bible Actually Says

CHIP INGRAM
WITH LANCE WITT

BakerBooks

a division of Baker Publishing Group
Grand Rapids, Michigan

Published by Baker Books
a division of Baker Publishing Group
P.O. Box 6287, Grand Rapids, MI 49516-6287
www.bakerbooks.com

Printed in the United States of America

Library of Congress Cataloging-in-Publication Data

ISBN 978-0-8010-1613-4 (cloth)
ISBN 978-0-8010-1914-2 (ITPE)

Published in association with Yates & Yates, www.yates2.com.

16 17 18 19 20 21 22   7 6 5 4 3 2 1

In keeping with biblical principles of creation stewardship, Baker Publishing Group advocates the responsible use of our natural resources. As a member of the Green Press Initiative, our company uses recycled paper when possible. The text paper of this book is composed in part of post-consumer waste.

CONTENTS

INTRODUCTION

So why another book on Heaven? That's a fair question. And is it even possible to know anything about Heaven? After all, we don't have any video footage of Heaven. We don't have any astronauts who have landed there. We do have a number of people who claim to have been there. But who can we trust?

Just recently Alex Malarkey recanted his story about a Heaven encounter. His story, published by Tyndale House, was called *The Boy Who Came Back from Heaven*. The book allegedly described what happened while Alex was in a coma after a car accident with his dad, Kevin. He was six years old at the time, and his story of miracles, angels, and life beyond this world became very popular. Alex, now a teenager, wrote a brief open letter in which he states, "I did not die. I did not go to Heaven. . . . I said I went to Heaven because I thought it would get me attention."[1]

Yet in spite of all the questions and unknowns and retractions, we are still intrigued with Heaven. In the last couple of decades there has been a surge of interest in the afterlife. Historically, when life gets hard and uncertain and dangerous, people tend to give more thought to life beyond this life. When life is hard "down here," we tend to wonder what's "up there." Unless your head is buried in the sand, you can't possibly believe we are living in utopian conditions.

No one is any longer living with the illusion that science or medicine or education or Google or Apple is going to solve the problems that plague our planet. In spite of all our advances, every day we see and hear about people who are killed by disease, weather, terror, accidents, crime, and natural disaster. Every single day we are confronted with our mortality. And so, we wonder. We wonder what happens to us after we die. Do we just cease to exist? Or, somehow, do we actually live on past the grave?

In the past few years, all kinds of videos, interviews, articles, and movies have been released that seek to give us some insight into the afterlife. But more information doesn't always lead to greater clarity. More words do not always translate into more understanding. The truth is, the glut of content on this subject has led to a lot of confusion and uncertainty.

Many people's views about Heaven have been shaped by Hollywood and movies about the afterlife. And while these movies might be interesting and entertaining, what is the basis for their portrayal of Heaven? In the last decade we have been deluged with scores of books about the afterlife. Yet even a casual analysis reveals huge discrepancies in their views and perspective about Heaven—what it is like and who goes there—so we have to ask the same question. What is the basis for their portrayal of Heaven?

In addition to all the movies and books and articles, there has even been a flood of people who claim to have experienced death and then were brought back to life. Their testimonials of the afterlife have captured our attention. But their experiences and descriptions can be wildly different. How do we know who to believe? Whose opinion should we trust? Did they really die or was it a dream? Do people simply psychologically "fill in" their near-death experiences (NDEs) with their previous worldview? Why do some see tunnels of light and others tunnels of darkness? To put it bluntly, on what authority do all these people speak? How do we know who is credible and who is not? For years, many people believed Alex Malarkey. And how do you reconcile experiences that contradict one another?

It is easy to see why there is so much confusion about Heaven.

Unlike math or science, there is no empirical evidence about Heaven. There is no equation that proves its existence. You can't put it in a test tube or place it under a microscope. So how do we know what's true? Is there anybody we can go to who is a reliable authority on the topic? Or are we just left with vague speculation and conjecture?

Behind any discussion about Heaven is the core issue of "authority." Upon what do we place our beliefs and hopes and declarations about Heaven? As followers of Jesus, we unashamedly anchor all of our beliefs and hopes in the unchanging and eternal Word of God. And by the way, our belief in the Bible as true and authoritative is not just wishful thinking. There is credible evidence that the Bible is what it claims to be: God-inspired and God-breathed.

If you haven't yet settled your own view of Scripture, I want to encourage you to explore it for yourself. It has stood the test of time and the scrutiny of critics. (For more on this, see Appendix A: "Why I Believe the Bible.")

This book is based on the foundational premise that the one person who has authority to speak about Heaven is the One who created it.

After Alex Malarkey recanted his story of going to Heaven, here was his insightful comment: "When I made the claims that I did, I had never read the Bible. People have profited from lies, and continue to. They should read the Bible, which is enough. The Bible is the only source of truth. Anything written by man cannot be infallible."[2]

So in these chapters we are going to systematically cut through all of the clutter, white noise, and conjecture about Heaven. And I will attempt to answer the question, What does the Bible say about the place called Heaven?

In the following pages you will discover a simple, clear, practical, and Biblical view of God's greatest hope and promise for His children . . . HEAVEN.

1

DOES HEAVEN *REALLY* MATTER?

Set your minds on things above, not on earthly things. For you died, and your life is now hidden with Christ in God. When Christ, who is your life, appears, then you also will appear with him in glory.

Colossians 3:2–4

'm afraid to die." Those were words I never expected to hear roll off my dad's lips. My father was a rugged, tough Marine who had been in combat in World War II. Although he was not quite seventeen, his mother signed for him to enter the war and help his country. He was strong and athletic and was assigned as a 50-caliber machine gunner in Guam and Iwo Jima. He rarely spoke of the horrors of war, but on two specific occasions, he shared the guilt he felt of killing thousands of men and the guilt of being wounded in Iwo Jima and being carried out while his fellow Marines died in combat.

He had seen fear in the eyes of other men, and I am sure he had battled it in his own heart. When he came home, the impact of the war manifested itself in subtle but real ways. I can remember him often getting up in the night just to be sure every door in the house was locked. He had been through so much and had witnessed the unspeakable evils of war. His casual beer consumption turned into an adult alcohol addiction that helped him deal with the pain and trauma of his past. It would forever mark his life.

In his later years my dad contracted a rare disease called Shy-Drager syndrome. This unusual disease is like Parkinson's, MS, and ALS all wrapped up into one. Over the previous few years we had watched my dad's physical health deteriorate as he battled this terrible disease. He went from having trouble walking to being confined to a wheelchair to ultimately being unable to get out of bed.

My dad did not come to Christ until he was in his fifties, but when he did, his life was thoroughly changed. And yet, as the reality of death began to sink in, this rugged Marine began to struggle with fear. One day as I was sitting next to his bed, he said, "I am afraid to die. I know I have a relationship with God and I know my sins are forgiven. But when I think about Heaven, it's just a blank." For my dad, Heaven was not a place of hope and comfort but was merely abstract, vague, and ethereal. Although he was confident that Jesus was going to be there and he knew that the alternative to Heaven wasn't good, there was nothing about the thought of Heaven that brought deep peace or alleviated his fear of dying. Even though my dad was a believer, the idea of Heaven was so elusive and foggy that it didn't bring him any comfort. I suspect that is true for many people.

My dad's experience and fear was a wake-up call for me as a son and as a pastor. I wasn't able in that moment to quickly and clearly articulate what Heaven is like and what people will experience in Heaven. I had studied the Bible and taught many topics, but Heaven wasn't one of them. The truth is, my perspective of Heaven was not too much different than my dad's. I was certainly aware of key passages about Heaven, but I did not have a cohesive and thorough

For my dad, Heaven was not a place of hope and comfort but was merely abstract, vague, and ethereal.

understanding of it. As my mind went back to my seminary days, I realized we never really spent much time learning about Heaven.

And so, not knowing how to comfort my dad, I decided to give him a book about heaven. My dad was very interested in the book, and at first he would read the book for himself. But eventually he got so sick he couldn't sit up and read. So his wife, Evelyn, would sit by his bedside and read to him.

I vividly remember coming back to visit my dad in his final days and observing a dramatic change in his outlook. The book helped Dad get a grasp of what Heaven is really going to be like. The truth about Heaven from God's Word turned Dad's fear into positive expectation.

While I was in his hospital room, a nurse came in and was talking to him about what they might need to do to extend his life. She wanted him to know his options, and she wanted to know his wishes about being resuscitated. And without any hesitation, he said, "Lady, no matter what happens, don't use any extreme means to keep me alive. Don't resuscitate me. Here's what I want you to know—I'm going to Heaven and it's going to be great." An unbelievable transformation had taken place. There was no fear and uncertainty. There was no panic or anxiety. There was only confidence and clarity. You see, my dad now had a deep assurance about Heaven. And that brought hope and comfort and made a huge difference in his last days.

That experience in many ways was a catalyst for my own journey of discovering what the Bible actually teaches about Heaven. And to my delight, and the encouragement of countless others, my discovery led to teaching about an amazing and wonderful place that God has prepared for us.

As we begin this study on Heaven, I want to ask you a few questions:

- How often do you think about Heaven?

- How many times this last week did Heaven cross your mind?

- When was the last time Heaven actually came up in a conversation?

- When was the last time you heard a sermon on Heaven?

- Do you have a Biblically informed view of Heaven?

While people are intrigued about the afterlife, my suspicion is that most of us really don't give it much thought or serious investigation.

Right now I want you to imagine walking into a hospital room. You can probably picture in your mind what it is like to walk down that hall past the nurses' station. You feel a little uneasy. You don't like hospitals. But on this day you have come to the hospital to visit your adolescent nephew who is dying from leukemia. You sit by his bedside and make small talk for a few minutes. But then, in the middle of your conversation he looks up at you from his hospital bed and asks, "Can you tell me what is going to happen to me after I die? Can you

"Can you tell me what is going to happen to me after I die? Can you explain to me what Heaven is going to be like?"

explain to me what Heaven is going to be like?" You are stopped dead in your tracks. In that moment, what would you say? I hope you'd do a better job explaining Heaven than I did with my dad, but my fear is that most of us don't have a clear understanding of what the Bible teaches.

Once we get past the "no more tears, no more sorrow, and Jesus will be there," we are often left with just a few random thoughts about Heaven and struggle to articulate what the Bible actually teaches about it. Even though we know we are going to die and even though we know it is the place where believers will spend eternity, most of us don't give it much thought. We seem to have more interest in where we are going for lunch than where we are going for eternity. For many of us, much like my dad, Heaven seems like a vague, mystical place that has little impact on our life today. Even though our life "here and now" often drowns out our thoughts about Heaven, I would like to challenge you to go on a journey with me to discover what Heaven is really like. I think you'll be pleasantly surprised at how a clear picture of your tomorrows will transform how you live your todays.

In fact, as archaeologists have studied ancient cultures and civilizations, one of their discoveries is that virtually every culture that has ever existed believes in an afterlife. There is something in our DNA that knows that this life is not all there is. In the book of Ecclesiastes, Solomon says that *"[God] has also set eternity in the human heart"* (3:11). God has planted inside of us an intuitive knowledge that there is life after death. The question is, what is that life like?

> **We seem to have more interest in where we are going for lunch than where we are going for eternity.**

As we begin this journey together to discover what the Bible actually teaches about Heaven, I want to warn you that you are in for some shocking new information—Heaven is NOT what you think, and it is better than you imagined.

The mental picture most of us have of Heaven far more resembles a Hollywood movie scene than it does the teachings of Scripture. In fact, let me just ask you, when you think of Heaven, what comes to mind? What images do you see? If you are like the overwhelming majority of Christians, your ideas have little connection to the Bible's portrayal of Heaven.

So, the question we are going to ask and answer is this: What does the Bible actually say about Heaven? Our focus is not going to be on what other books say or what movies portray or what some person has experienced in a near-death encounter. We are going to laser focus on what God has to say about Heaven.

Before we dig into Scripture to discover what God has to say about Heaven, let's first answer the question, why study Heaven? Let me give you three reasons why this topic is important and relevant for us.

Three Reasons to Study Heaven

1. Our misconceptions are crippling us.

Most of us carry around some distorted views and false thinking about Heaven. We tend to believe we really can't know much about it. Certainly there are things about Heaven we won't know until we get there. But the Bible provides far more information about Heaven than most of us realize. And the Bible's description of Heaven is radically different than our Hollywood-infused images that we carry around in our minds.

Another misconception we carry around is that Heaven is an otherworldly experience, totally disconnected and different than anything we experience here in this life. We picture disembodied spirits that float around and play harps all day. And maybe like Clarence from the movie *It's a Wonderful Life*, you think we are going to be earning our wings. Or maybe from some other movie, you think Heaven has no buildings or structures or furniture. Heaven is filled with wispy clouds, and apparently colors aren't allowed there, because everyone is wearing white. And obviously in Heaven there is no fashion because everyone wears a loose-fitting white robe. There are no belts, scarves, earrings, bracelets, vests, sweaters, or pants in Heaven. And Heaven must have a mega fog machine, because as you may have noticed in the movies, you never see anyone's feet in Heaven—the floor of Heaven is always covered with a layer of fog. I think these otherworldly portrayals of Heaven cause us to dismiss any serious consideration of it.

Another misconception held by many Christians is that Heaven is one really long church service. I'm a pastor, and as much as I enjoy great sermons and great worship music, the thought of Heaven being a really long church service sounds terribly boring. No wonder so many Christians don't seem all that interested in Heaven.

As I've spoken to students about Jesus coming again and the prospects of Heaven, some of them have said to me, "I don't want Jesus to come back until I get married and have sex."

I've also talked with an older couple who were planning a trip to Hawaii who said, "I don't want Jesus to come back until after our Hawaii trip."

We don't really know what Heaven is like, but we are pretty sure it can't be better than marriage, sex, or Hawaii.

When we carry these misconceptions around in our mind, the results are very predictable. We tend to live with a very temporal perspective rather than an eternal one. We unconsciously fix our energy on the here and now. We live for today and focus on the life we've been given here. This is in stark contrast to how most Christians lived in the first 2,000 years of the church's existence. Heaven was a central topic of teaching and discussion. It was also a central theme of Christian songs and worship music. But that has radically shifted in the last hundred years.

> We don't really know what Heaven is like, but we are pretty sure it can't be better than marriage, sex, or Hawaii.

As strange as it sounds, one of the barriers we have to maintaining an eternal perspective is that we have it pretty good in this life. As we have gotten more comfortable with life "here" (earth), we have less desire for life "there" (Heaven). We can tend to live as though we believe this life is all there is and that it will go on forever. We know that's not true intellectually, but under the pressures and demands of this world, I find that we lose sight of the next. When my dad died and when my wife won her battle with breast cancer, I was powerfully reminded that everything about this life is fragile, vulnerable, and temporal.

No one knows the future. We could be days away from the next recession, terrorist attack, or natural disaster. The stock market could take a great dip or your company could downsize tomorrow. Car accidents, heart attacks, and cancer seem to be no respecter of persons. There is so much in this life that you and I simply can't control.

But when life comes unraveled and I am confronted with my mortality, all of a sudden the topic of Heaven becomes very relevant. When my secure and stable life intersects with crisis and tragedy, it can be a jarring experience. It is a sobering reminder that I am not guaranteed tomorrow. When you meet people who have cancer, or you talk with people who have debilitating diseases, or you travel to third world countries where people live in abject poverty, you discover that they think about Heaven a lot more than we do.

Since life is pretty stable for most of us, our view of Heaven is some version of a vague, mystical, boring place that we don't tend to think about much and have rarely studied. I have never taken a formal survey, but from my thirty years as a pastor, I can tell you that apart from some crisis, most North American Christians in general are not excited about or longing for Heaven. My hope is that this book will spark something deep inside you that turns your thoughts and desires toward Heaven like never before.

You know that feeling you have when you come home after a long trip? You're exhausted from all the travel and from sleeping in hotel beds. Then you pull into your driveway, walk in the front door, drop your suitcase, and think to yourself, *It is so good to be home.* Your body relaxes and you can feel the stress melt away. Coming home brings a sense of relief and joy and relaxation and peace. Like Dorothy says in *The Wizard of Oz,* "There's no place like home."[3] Well, multiply that a million times and you begin to get a glimmer of what Heaven will really be like.

Unfortunately, if we don't understand this and continue to carry around misconceptions about Heaven, we will have little interest in it. The result is tragic. If my ultimate hope is not in Heaven, then I begin to ask this world and the people in it to come through for me in ways that will never happen. Frustration and disappointment with God, marriage, family, friends, and my job are inevitable. That's why the Scripture commands us to think accurately and clearly about Heaven.

2. We are commanded to think about Heaven.

It's not just a good suggestion or a nice idea.

> Since, then, you have been raised with Christ, set your hearts on things above, where Christ is, seated at the right hand of God. Set your minds on things above, not on earthly things. For you died, and your life is now hidden with Christ in God. When Christ, who is your life, appears, then you also will appear with him in glory.
>
> Colossians 3:1–4

Notice that the apostle Paul gives us two different commands in this short passage. We are commanded to set our hearts on "things above" and we are commanded to set our minds on "things above." God's commands are always for our benefit, and

23

when we obey them, we receive grace and experience His peace. A command requires us to willfully choose to do something. For most of us, our minds and hearts are set on the things of this life. The world's pressures and enticements dominate our hearts and minds. As a result, we are preoccupied with things that are temporal.

Last week I had breakfast with a forty-three-year-old executive at Google. He's strong and athletic, has a great wife and four kids, and just learned he has stage 3 cancer. I had been sick for two weeks, was behind on my message preparation, working on this book, and had a less-than-positive attitude . . . until I heard that word "cancer." My petty issues and pressures evaporated almost instantly as I stepped into his world and what really matters.

Much of our anxiety and lack of peace and struggle in this life is the result of not having a clear understanding of Heaven and an eternal perspective that comes from our hope in the life to come. Studying Heaven has practical implications for my life here and now. A clear understanding of Heaven results in a longing for Heaven, which empowers me to make wise decisions about my priorities in this life.

The third reason we should study Heaven is the most sobering reason of all.

3. A faulty view of Heaven destines us to a wasted life on Earth.

If that statement is true, then our study of Heaven becomes even more critical.

To help you understand this, I want to take you to the book of John. Jesus is spending His last night with the disciples before He will be betrayed and ultimately crucified. He has spent the last three years preparing these men to take over when He is gone. In John 13 Jesus has now washed the feet of the disciples and they have shared the Lord's Supper together. Judas is now en route to betray Jesus. Jesus is sitting there with eleven ordinary men who will transform the world. So, what would He say to them? If you were Jesus and this was your last chance to address the troops, what would you talk about? Would you share the strategic plan for kingdom impact? Would you talk about the organizational chart for the disciples and who is to be in charge? Would you talk about the church and the priorities the church should have? What would you say if you were Jesus?

> **A clear understanding of Heaven results in a longing for Heaven, which empowers me to make wise decisions about my priorities in this life.**

He knows what lies ahead for these men. He knows they are going to be rejected and persecuted. He knows every one of them except one would be martyred for their faith. He knows they are going to take the message of Christ into areas that are hostile to the gospel. He knows that it will be hard on their families. In light of that reality, what words would Jesus leave them with?

We don't have to wonder. We know exactly what Jesus told them in that moment:

> Do not let your hearts be troubled. You believe in God; believe also in me. My Father's house has many rooms; if that were not so, would I have told you that I am going there to prepare a place for you? And if I go and prepare a place for you, I will come back and take you to be with me that you also may be where I am. (John 14:1–3)

Jesus knew that a crystal clear view of eternity and of their future home in Heaven would sustain them through the most difficult of times. When life would get hard and when persecution would come, the hope of Heaven would motivate them to persevere. As Hebrews says, they were waiting for a heavenly city that God was building. And it wasn't some ethereal, vague place with a lot of fog and white robes. Their sense of Heaven was clear and real and tangible and attractive.

If Heaven is so important to Jesus and we are commanded to think about Heaven, how did we get so misinformed in the last hundred years?

- The father of lies wants us to get sucked into a world system that he is behind.

John 8:44 says that Satan is a liar and is the father of lies. He is a master of deception. Satan doesn't want you to have a clear picture of all that God has planned for you in eternity. So if he can get you to think that you will be floating around on clouds and playing a harp in Heaven, there isn't a chance you will take it very seriously. Or if he can get you to think Heaven is a long, boring worship service, he knows there won't be any longing for a place like that. Or if the devil can get you to think that this world is where the good life is, then he knows you won't spend much time thinking about Heaven.

- Our theological training has lacked any serious emphasis and focus on Heaven.

I went back to some of my classic theology books. Most every evangelical pastor would have these on their shelves or at least be familiar with them. In one six-volume systematic theology set, there are two pages on the New Heaven and the New Earth. In the 737 pages of Berkhof's theology book, one page is dedicated to the New Heaven and New Earth. In Baxter's classic and very thick work called *Explore the Book*, there are about four pages dedicated to Heaven and eternity. A well-thought-through doctrine of Heaven is largely absent from some of our greatest theological works.

> **Jesus knew that a crystal clear view of eternity and of their future home in Heaven would sustain them through the most difficult of times.**

As a result, pastors like me weren't really taught much about Heaven. We learned about the various views of the end of times (eschatology), but almost nothing about Heaven itself.

Therefore, there hasn't been much teaching on Heaven to our congregations. Our focus has almost exclusively been on helping people live successfully in this temporal world rather than being prepared for the eternal world.

Add to that a contemporary culture that is all about "now." We want instant everything. We don't like to wait, and delayed gratification has become a foreign concept.

Our distorted view of Heaven has led to a distorted view of this life. I want to suggest that one of the major reasons temptation is so hard to resist and our priorities are so skewed and we are so seduced by the world is because we have no real idea of what Heaven is really like. Understanding Biblical truth about Heaven has very practical implications.

So I want to invite you on a journey to discover what God says about Heaven. It will change your perspective. It will change your desires. It will change your priorities. *IT WILL CHANGE YOUR LIFE.*

2

WHAT'S *REALLY* TRUE ABOUT HEAVEN?

My Father's house has many rooms; if that were not so, would I have told you that I am going there to prepare a place for you? And if I go and prepare a place for you, I will come back and take you to be with me that you also may be where I am.

John 14:2–3

When my grandmother was a little girl, she came to America on a long boat ride from Scotland. Her maiden name was McGregor and her Scottish roots ran deep. There were certain American words she refused to use and a few Scottish ones that baffled me.

As a young boy, I was assigned to help Grandma get ready for her visit to our home. I'll never forget the first time she told me to get her "grip." I asked Grandma to repeat what she said, because I assumed I didn't hear her correctly. Then she motioned to me to get her "grip" and put it in the car. Still puzzled, I walked near where she was pointing and asked her yet again what she wanted.

Now frustrated, Grandma walked over to her small suitcase, looked at me as though I was deaf, and placed it in my hands with the exhortation, "Put my 'grip' in the car so we can get going." This funny childhood memory reminds me of why there is so much confusion about Heaven.

As you know, words can have multiple meanings. For example, the word "point" can refer to the point of a pencil or using your finger to point to something or making a point in a debate. The word "right" can refer to a right turn or doing the right thing. Well, in the same way, the word "Heaven" can have multiple meanings. And if we are going to get an accurate understanding of what the Bible has to say about Heaven, our journey must begin with the word "Heaven." In the Bible, the word "Heaven" is used to describe three different places.

Heaven's Meanings

Sky

Stars

Abode of God

First, the word "Heaven" is used to describe the atmosphere or the sky. *Second*, the word "Heaven" is used when talking about the stars and the sun and the universe. In Psalm 19:1, David says, *"The heavens declare the glory of God; the skies proclaim the work of his hands."* Later in that same chapter David declares, *"In the heavens God has pitched a tent for the sun"* (v. 4). *Third*, the word "Heaven" is used to describe the abode of God. It is the place where God resides, and this usage is primarily where we are going to focus.

In Revelation chapters 4 and 5, John speaks of the throne of God, which is obviously a reference to God's rule and dominion. But it is also a reference to the place where God abides. Now, we know that God is omnipresent. He is not limited to Heaven. His presence can be found anywhere and everywhere.

For example, in Solomon's prayer of dedication for the temple, he prays, *"But will God really dwell on earth? The heavens, even the highest heaven, cannot contain you. How much less this temple I have built!"* (1 Kings 8:27). Or listen to David's prayer in Psalm 139:7–10, when he speaks of God's omnipresence.

> Where can I go from your Spirit?
>> Where can I flee from your presence?
> If I go up to the heavens, you are there;
>> if I make my bed in the depths, you are there.
> If I rise on the wings of the dawn,
>> if I settle on the far side of the sea,
> even there your hand will guide me,
>> your right hand will hold me fast.

However, the place where God resides and where there is no sin and where He is seen in all of His glory . . . that is HEAVEN. In the chapters ahead we will learn about the present (or Intermediate) Heaven, about what happens to us immediately after we die, and about the New Heaven that will be on the New Earth that God has prepared for us. But since this topic has caused so much confusion, let's start with the basics.

The Bible is full of promises about this place called Heaven. So let's discover some *general truths* about Heaven *that come straight from the Scripture*. We'll begin with an overview of these truths, and in later chapters, these concepts will be fully developed.

1. Heaven is a real, tangible place (John 14).

Heaven is not a theoretical concept or a state of mind. It is not make-believe or pretend or a figment of somebody's imagination. Just like Miami and London and Tokyo are actual places, Heaven is a real and actual place. In John 14, Jesus told the disciples that He was going to prepare a "place" for them. He wasn't going to prepare a state of mind. He wasn't going to prepare a concept. No, He was going to prepare an actual place specially created for those who have a personal relationship with God.

> My Father's house has many rooms; if that were not so, would I have told you that I am going there to prepare a place for you? And if I go and prepare a place for you, I will come back and

take you to be with me that you also may be where I am. You know the way to the place where I am going. (vv. 2–4)

Notice first that Jesus refers to His Father's house and that His house has many rooms in it. Second, notice that three different times in this short passage Jesus uses the word "place." The word translated "place" has been referred to as mansions in some translations, but the reference was to rooms that were added on to the patriarch's house as sons married and brought their wives to live in the extended family compound or estate. Lastly, notice that Jesus says He is coming back to get us so

> **Jesus wasn't going to prepare a state of mind. He wasn't going to prepare a concept. No, He was going to prepare an actual place.**

that we can be with Him. So, if Jesus is real and He resides in some PLACE, then we are promised to be in that place with Him.

2. God the Father is there (Matt. 6:9) and Jesus is at His right hand (Rom. 8:34).

In Jesus' model prayer in the Sermon on the Mount, He taught the disciples to begin their prayers by addressing "Our Father in Heaven." According to Romans 8, after Jesus was crucified and resurrected, He ascended back into Heaven and is at the right hand of God interceding for us. In Acts 7, when Stephen

33

was stoned, the Bible says that he saw Heaven opened up and Jesus standing at the right hand of God.

Jesus is the one person who experienced Heaven prior to being born on this planet. So, when He talks about Heaven and eternity, He speaks with authority and credibility.

3. All believers are there (Heb. 12:23).

Hebrews 12 talks about "the church of the firstborn." This is a reference to the church that belongs to Jesus, the firstborn of God. The church of Jesus Christ is made up of all believers who have put their faith and trust in Christ. Following the statement about the church of the firstborn, the writer of Hebrews says that the names of all believers are written in Heaven.

4. There will be people in Heaven from every nation.

And they sang a new song, saying:

> "You are worthy to take the scroll
>   and to open its seals,
> because you were slain,
>   and with your blood you purchased for God
>   persons from every tribe and language and people
>   and nation.
> You have made them to be a kingdom and priests to
>   serve our God,
>   and they will reign on the earth." (Rev. 5:9–10)

In this great scene around the throne in Heaven, the four living creatures and twenty-four elders declare that Jesus alone is worthy to open the seals of the scroll that would reveal these end-time events. The sinless sacrifice of Jesus on the cross is what made it possible for people from every nation to respond to the gospel and have a place in Heaven.

This is a great picture of the heart of God. Heaven will be multiethnic, with individuals representing every culture and people group and nation around the throne of God.

5. Our names are recorded there (Luke 10:20).

Something very interesting happens in Luke 10. Jesus sent out seventy-two of His followers two by two into the surrounding towns and villages. They were to heal the sick and spread the good news about Jesus. When the seventy-two returned, the Bible says they were filled with joy and said, *"Lord, even the demons submit to us in your name"* (v. 17). This was the precursor to a mission trip debrief. And to their shock and delight, these early followers of Jesus found that they even had power and authority over demons.

> **Heaven will be multiethnic, with individuals representing every culture and people group and nation.**

Jesus was quick to warn them. He said, *"Do not rejoice that the spirits submit to you, but rejoice that your names are written*

35

in heaven" (v. 20). It's like Jesus was saying, "As great as it is that you have authority over demons, don't ever forget that the greatest gift you've been given is that your name is written in Heaven."

Have you ever had the experience of attending a conference and having to go to the registration booth? At the registration booth you get your name tag and conference materials. You give the conference staff your name and they scan the list of people who have registered. And after a few seconds they say, "Mr. Ingram, we found your name." And then they proceed to hand you your name badge. You see, having your name written on the list says that you belong. It says that you have a right to enter and to participate. It says that you took the necessary steps to have a seat at the conference. It says that you meet the qualifications for entry. The same is true with Heaven. The fact that your name is written there means that as one who has put your trust in Jesus, you belong and you have the authority to enter and to participate.

> **The greatest gift you've been given is that your name is written in Heaven.**

6. We have an inheritance there (1 Pet. 1:3–4).

In 1 Peter 1 we find this amazing promise:

> Praise be to the God and Father of our Lord Jesus Christ! In his great mercy he has given us new birth into a living hope

through the resurrection of Jesus Christ from the dead, and into an inheritance that can never perish, spoil or fade. This inheritance is kept in heaven for you. (vv. 3–4)

I want you to take a moment and try to imagine that your dad is a billionaire. (I don't know about you, but that is hard to imagine.) And one day he walks in and announces that he is leaving his entire fortune to you. Now, that is pretty fun to imagine. I am going to bet your heart would start beating a little faster, a smile would come across your face, and you would get downright excited about all that was coming your way. Here's the good news: your heavenly Father has promised you an eternal inheritance and it is stored in Heaven for safekeeping. That's not just a warm fuzzy theological thought. What is actually coming your way in eternity far exceeds inheriting a billion dollars.

7. Our citizenship is there (Phil. 3:20).

In Philippians 3:20, the apostle Paul says, *"But our citizenship is in heaven. And we eagerly await a Savior from there, the Lord Jesus Christ."*

There is an old song that says, "This world is not our home," and that is absolutely true. The Bible says that we are pilgrims and nomads only passing through this land called earth. That's one reason why we shouldn't put our roots down too deeply in this world.

Think about it this way: our American ambassador to Japan might have a temporary residence there, but even in that foreign land he is an American citizen. To abandon his US citizenship would be a kind of treason. For Christians to live and act as citizens of this world is spiritual treason. In 2 Corinthians Paul says that we are ambassadors who are here representing our king. But our citizenship is in a different kingdom. We belong to the kingdom of Heaven. And as citizens of the heavenly kingdom, there are privileges and blessings that belong to me simply because I am a citizen. I know it's hard to grasp, but you have a spiritual passport you received when you trusted Christ as your Savior, and your homeland is Heaven. God expects us to act accordingly.

8. Specific eternal rewards are given there (Matt. 6:19–21).

Did you know that what you do in this life has impact on your life in Heaven? In the Sermon on the Mount, Jesus provided wise advice and a clear challenge with these words:

> Do not store up for yourselves treasures on earth, where moths and vermin destroy, and where thieves break in and steal. But store up for yourselves treasures in heaven, where moths and vermin do not destroy, and where thieves do not break in and steal. For where your treasure is, there your heart will be also. (Matt. 6:19–21)

Jesus gives us a sobering reminder that the stuff of this world is temporary. It will wear out, give out, break down, and ultimately be thrown in the trash. That new car you want so badly is only going to last for a few years. That new smartphone you have been craving will be outdated less than a year from now. That jacket you've been eyeing will sit unnoticed in the back of your closet by next winter.

But the treasures we store up in Heaven are eternal and will never rot, rust, or ruin. By the kind of life I live now, I can send treasure on to Heaven. When I make financial investments or put money in my 401(k), I am putting money away that will be there for me later in life. The same is true spiritually. When I make spiritual investments of my time, talents, and treasure in God's kingdom and His purpose, I am making deposits in Heaven that will be waiting for me when I arrive.

9. It's the best of earth, only better (Rev. 22).

Contrary to popular culture and the last five movies about Heaven, we're not going to be floating in clouds wearing white robes and playing harps. Heaven is very tangible and real. The world we now live in is an old earth that is fallen. But there is coming a New Heaven and a New Earth that is as real, physical, and tangible as this earth.

But it will be infinitely better. It won't be marred by sin and disease and pollution and disaster. The planet we live on is a gift from God, but it is stained and scarred by sin. No scientific or environmental breakthrough is going to make this a paradise. We must be good stewards of the planet God has given us, but we shouldn't put our hope here. God is preparing for us a New Heaven and a New Earth that far exceeds our wildest imagination.

10. Sin, death, and sorrow are absent (Rev. 21:4).

Heaven will be great because a few things *won't* be there. In Revelation 21:4, John says, *"'He will wipe every tear from their eyes. There will be no more death' or mourning or crying or pain, for the old order of things has passed away."*

I have shared this passage many times over the years to comfort families at the loss of a loved one. In those moments when death is so palpable, I remind believers that the death of their loved one ushers them to a place where no more death or pain or fears will be allowed. But when you are staring at a casket and you feel that sense of loss, you are reminded that in this world death and disease are real and painful. And no one is exempt. There is no place you can go on this earth to escape the clutches of death.

You see, the truth is that we are all "terminal." The death rate in your community is 100 percent. None of us are exempt and none of us will escape. Ecclesiastes 8:8 (NLT) says, *"None of us can hold back our spirit from departing. None of us has the power to prevent the day of our death."*

We are all "terminal." The death rate in your community is 100 percent.

So, the question is not so much "if," but "when." The Scripture says that the Lord has numbered our days, but He has never revealed His spreadsheet. I don't know the number of my days and you don't know the number of yours. But one thing we do know for sure is that death is coming. If for any reason you're not certain that you would go to Heaven when you die, I encourage you to skip to the beginning of chapter 11 and learn for certain that Heaven will be yours.

In stark contrast to earth, Heaven will be very different. Sin and death and sorrow will be forever removed. Imagine a place where there are no cemeteries or funeral homes. Imagine a place where there are no rehab and recovery clinics. God is preparing that place for us right now.

11. Adventure, work, discovery, and rulership await us (Rev. 22).

Adventure and work are not things we usually associate with Heaven. What a contrast to the idea that Heaven is only an ethereal experience of disembodied spirits. Or what a contrast to the notion that Heaven is sitting for eternity through a really long church service. There will be activity and work to be done. We will be productive, and there will be adventure and new experiences. We will learn, work, and create. Songs will be written. Art, music, and culture will be created as we continue to learn of the infinite wisdom and glory of God.

When you start to grasp these realities, Heaven starts to sound like a place we would want to go to. Perhaps it was Paul's clear and deep understanding of Heaven that created in him such a desire for it.

In the book of Philippians, the apostle Paul finds himself in conflict. Even though he was in prison and there was a good chance that he was going to be executed, we don't hear any sense of fear in his words. What we do hear is Paul battling the conflicting emotions of wanting to go to Heaven to be with God and yet feeling the need to stay around and help these Philippian Christians:

> For to me, to live is Christ and to die is gain. If I am to go on living in the body, this will mean fruitful labor for me. Yet what shall I choose? I do not know! I am torn between the two: I desire to depart and be with Christ, which is better by far; but it is more necessary for you that I remain in the body. (Phil. 1:21–24)

Paul says to die is "gain" and if he departs this life he will be with Christ. The apostle's view of Heaven was so clear and so positively compelling that he even says it is his desire to depart this earth and be with Christ.

So, let me ask you: What's your view of Heaven? Does your mind think about Heaven and provide you the kind of hope that it did for Paul?

As we close this chapter, notice the clear teaching from Scripture that death for a believer is nothing more than the immediate transition into the presence of God. Paul's words confirm that this life is not all there is. There is life after we die, and if we are believers, that life is in the presence of Christ. The life awaiting us in Heaven is beyond our wildest dreams and imaginations.

3

WHERE DID HEAVEN *REALLY* BEGIN?

Then the LORD God formed a man from the dust of the ground and breathed into his nostrils the breath of life, and the man became a living being. Now the LORD God had planted a garden in the east, in Eden; and there he put the man he had formed.

Genesis 2:7–8

When we think about Heaven, we almost always gravitate in our minds to "up there" or "someday in the future" when we will be with God forever. Those concepts are normal and natural, but not altogether accurate. If Heaven is the abode of God (where He lives and reigns in a perfect environment) and it is a place He ultimately wants to share with us, maybe a look back at the Garden of Eden will help us get a more accurate picture of the ultimate New Heaven and New Earth God is preparing for us.

Let me begin with a statement that might shock you: Heaven is perfect, but incomplete. That statement might sound a little odd and even heretical, but it is absolutely true. There is something missing, or maybe it is better to say there is "someone" missing. As a dad, I know what it is like to anxiously wait on my kids to get home. When my kids were growing up, each of them had their own place in our home. They had their own room and they had refrigerator rights at our house. Because they carried the Ingram name, they could just walk in the front door, without knocking or without permission.

Even when they were away from home, I wanted them to be protected and provided for. I wanted them to enjoy their friends and serve others. I was intimately interested in how they lived when they were not at home, but as a dad I longed for them to be home.

Having a room for them is not the same as being with them. Proximity matters. There are certain aspects of relationship that you can't fully enjoy unless you are together.

That, my friend, is a picture of Heaven. Above everything, our heavenly Father longs to be with us. He can't wait for us to come home and be with Him. As a child of God, you already have a place prepared for you there. You carry the family name and so you belong there. But Heaven isn't complete until you "come home."

So, in order to understand more about our future home, we need to get an overarching understanding of the story of God as recorded in the Bible. Again, I want to remind you to think of Heaven as primarily the abode of God, not so much as the place Christians go when they die. Every time you read the word "Heaven," see it primarily as the place where God is.

With that in view, where is the first place we see God and mankind in a perfect environment? If you're thinking the Garden of Eden, you're 100 percent right. The Garden of Eden was a kind of Heaven on earth. God, in His goodness and generosity, created a perfect paradise. It was beautiful, abundant, fruitful, and perfect. There were no tsunamis,

> **Heaven isn't complete until you "come home."**

earthquakes, or hurricanes. And there was no pollution or global warming. Everything was in perfect balance. As you slowly read the words below, notice the goodness and graciousness of God.

Then God said, "Let us make mankind in our image, in our likeness, so that they may rule over the fish in the sea and the birds in the sky, over the livestock and all the wild animals, and over all the creatures that move along the ground."

So God created mankind in his own image,
in the image of God he created them;
male and female he created them.

God blessed them and said to them, "Be fruitful and increase in number; fill the earth and subdue it. Rule over the fish in the sea and the birds in the sky and over every living creature that moves on the ground."

Then God said, "I give you every seed-bearing plant on the face of the whole earth and every tree that has fruit with seed in it. They will be yours for food. And to all the beasts of the earth and all the birds in the sky and all the creatures that move along the ground—everything that has the breath of life in it—I give every green plant for food." And it was so. (Gen. 1:26–30)

Notice that God gives Adam and Eve authority over all that He has created. Mankind is clearly the first, the highest, and most precious among all of God's creation. It is only mankind that is stamped with the image of God. I love how verse 28 starts with the words "God blessed them." It is the heart of God to bless and lavish us with things that are good for us and bring us delight.

God gives Adam and Eve the privilege of participating in the act of creation. He commands them to be fruitful and multiply. God could have just dropped fully formed humans out of Heaven, or He could have made more humans just like He did Adam and Eve. But He allows them the joy and privilege of procreation.

Then, in verse 29, God provides way above and beyond their basic needs. God gives them "every seed-bearing plant" and "every tree that has fruit." He lavishes them with abundance and with variety. And in verse 30 God blesses them with "every green plant for food." This is the mother of all salad bars. God delights in the happiness of His people.

As the crowning achievement of God's creation, He makes a man and a woman in His image. They are given the authority to rule over the rest of creation, and they are told to multiply and fill the earth. The only restriction God gave them was that they couldn't eat from the tree of the knowledge of good and evil. There was an abundance of blessing and only one rule. And even the one rule was motivated by God's love and goodness. God only puts fences around things that will hurt us.

Adam and Eve didn't just sit around all day. They were given the assignment of working the garden and taking care of it. They had purpose. Every need they could possibly have was provided for in the garden. This amazing place had been carefully crafted by a good God to be perfectly suited for Adam and Eve.

> **God only puts fences around things that will hurt us.**

Scientists have marveled for generations at how perfectly the earth was made for man. The earth's axis is tilted exactly 23.5 degrees and is just right to create the seasons. The tilt also prevents extreme heat and cold that would make our planet uninhabitable. The distance of the earth from the sun is sometimes referred to as the *Goldilocks zone*. It is not too far and it is not too close. We are just the right distance from the sun for humans to live on this planet. Our distance from the sun is exactly precise for water to exist as liquid, and of course water is essential for life to be sustained. The earth's size is just right to contain our atmosphere, which serves as kind of a blanket for the earth and provides just the right mixture of nitrogen (78 percent) and oxygen (21 percent) for us to live.

Truly this amazing planet created with such majesty and precision is a testimony of a good God who wanted just the right home for His children. Scientists have discovered over 200 conditions that all must be in place and in the right balance for life to exist. The earth is unique among all the galaxies that we have explored. It is a rare, perfect environment for life.[4]

In this perfect environment, God comes and communes with Adam and Eve. He wants to be with them and have a relationship with them. Usually when you hear about the Garden of Eden, the emphasis is on the garden. We often talk about this paradise that was perfect and beautiful. But the most beautiful thing about the garden was the relationship and "community" that Adam and Eve enjoyed with God.

> **Truly this amazing planet created with such majesty and precision is a testimony of a good God who wanted just the right home for His children.**

The garden was not an end in itself. The main purpose of the Garden of Eden was to provide a place where Adam and Eve could be in intimate, joyful relationship with God. The same God who spoke the universe into existence went to great trouble to create the earth as the one place humans could inhabit in that universe. Then He created Adam and Eve and gave them purpose and work and meaning. And God creates people in His image. He does all of that so that He could be in relationship with us.

When you read the first couple chapters of Genesis, it is helpful to think of a camera shot. Chapter 1 of Genesis looks at creation through a wide-angle lens. Chapter 2 looks at creation through a zoom lens.

After an overview of the creation process through the wide-angle lens, Genesis 2 zooms in on the specific creation of man:

> Then the LORD God formed a man from the dust of the ground and breathed into his nostrils the breath of life, and the man became a living being.
>
> Now the LORD God had planted a garden in the east, in Eden; and there he put the man he had formed. The LORD God made all kinds of trees grow out of the ground—trees that were pleasing to the eye and good for food. In the middle of the garden were the tree of life and the tree of the knowledge of good and evil.
>
> A river watering the garden flowed from Eden. (vv. 7–10)

Can you sense the heart of God in this passage? As a good and loving Father, He wants to create this wonderful place for His children. Notice the trees—there were all kinds. Have you ever noticed that our God is a creative God who loves variety? And the trees were pleasing to the eye. They weren't just functional, they were beautiful. We have a heavenly Father who loves beauty and splendor. And then He made trees that produced good food. He even went to the trouble to create things that would be pleasing to our taste buds. He created food that we would enjoy. God could have just created a kind of nourishment to

49

simply fuel our bodies, much like gasoline does for a car. But He created wide varieties of foods that would nourish us, and He gave us the great sensation of taste so we could actually enjoy the eating experience.

Then there is a river that runs through the garden. This goes way beyond the most beautiful resort you have ever seen.

As a further act of grace, God gives man work to do: *"The Lord God took the man and put him in the Garden of Eden to work it and take care of it"* (v. 15). God made us to find meaning and dignity through work. God wired into our DNA this need to co-create, to accomplish and be productive. People all the time talk about making a difference and finding their purpose or discovering their destiny. All of those statements are evidence that God made us to be useful. It's one of the reasons the Bible speaks so strongly about laziness. When we are lazy, we are squandering the gifts that God gave us. When we are lazy, God knows that we will be unfulfilled, because He made us to be helpful and productive difference-makers.

> **God wired into our DNA this need to co-create, to accomplish and be productive.**

But God also wired into us the need for relationship, not just with Him, but with other people. *"The Lord God said, 'It is not good for the man to be alone. I will make a helper suitable for him'"* (v. 18). This is the first time in the Bible we read the words "it is not good." What wasn't good is for man to be alone.

No giraffe or bear or even a dog could provide the kind of companionship that Adam needed. So, again, as a kind and benevolent Father, God creates a beautiful and exquisite companion for Adam, and she is called Eve.

> So the LORD God caused the man to fall into a deep sleep; and while he was sleeping, he took one of the man's ribs and then closed up the place with flesh. Then the LORD God made a woman from the rib he had taken out of the man, and he brought her to the man. (vv. 21–22)

The last verse of Genesis 2 says Adam and his wife were both naked, and they felt no shame.

There is no sin, no insecurity, no mixed motives, no comparing, no hypocrisy, and no using of people. They were completely transparent and vulnerable and it was good.

Now if you're wondering why I'm spending so much time analyzing the Garden of Eden in a book about Heaven, let me give you a clue. If you skip ahead from the end of Genesis 2 to the last two chapters of the Bible, you will discover a very similar scene to what we see in the Garden of Eden. There are beautiful trees and a river, and just like the Garden of Eden, it is perfect. Everything that gets destroyed between Genesis 3 and Revelation 20 gets restored when God brings a New Heaven and a New Earth. I want you to see the connection between Revelation 21 and 22 and Genesis 1 and 2. The New Heaven and the New Earth are not some ethereal place. They are the restoration and redemption of the very real place that God created in Genesis.

However, when you move to Genesis 3, sin now enters the world and everything changes.

> When the woman saw that the fruit of the tree was good for food and pleasing to the eye, and also desirable for gaining wisdom, she took some and ate it. She also gave some to her husband, who was with her, and he ate it. Then the eyes of both of them were opened, and they realized they were naked; so they sewed fig leaves together and made coverings for themselves.
>
> Then the man and his wife heard the sound of the LORD God as he was walking in the garden in the cool of the day, and they hid from the LORD God among the trees of the garden. But the LORD God called to the man, "Where are you?"
>
> He answered, "I heard you in the garden, and I was afraid because I was naked; so I hid." (vv. 6–10)

For the very first time, sin enters this perfect environment. This causes separation from God, and it will cause separation between Adam and Eve. He blames her and she blames the serpent. And God brings consequences to bear for their disobedience. First, He declares judgment on the serpent. And then there is the consequence that Eve will experience severe pain in childbirth. And for Adam the consequence is that work will now be hard and exhausting and full of constant challenge. He would no longer garden in a perfect environment, but he would have to deal with thorns and thistles the rest of his life. The thorns and thistles become a kind of metaphor that would foreshadow the hard things of life.

But even in the midst of God's judgment, there is mercy shown.

"The LORD *God made garments of skin for Adam and his wife and clothed them"* (v. 21). God provides for them even in their disobedience. This covering is a foreshadowing of the sacrifice of Jesus on the cross and how His blood covers our sins.

The chapter goes on to say,

> And the LORD God said, "The man has now become like one of us, knowing good and evil. He must not be allowed to reach out his hand and take also from the tree of life and eat, and live forever." (v. 22)

This may not seem like an act of mercy, but it absolutely is another sign of God's goodness. If Adam eats of the tree of life in this sinful state, he will stay separated from God forever. So, if you read the last couple verses of Genesis 3, you will discover that God sets a powerful cherubim on the east side of the garden to guard the tree of life. We know that what happens in Genesis 3 damages the perfect relationship between man and God. Only in the coming of Jesus and His death on the cross would it be possible for man to be reconciled to God.

But even in the midst of God's judgment, there is mercy shown.

Not only was man's relationship with God damaged, but sin's entrance into the world also affected creation.

> For the creation was subjected to frustration, not by its own choice, but by the will of the one who subjected it, in hope that

the creation itself will be liberated from its bondage to decay and brought into the freedom and glory of the children of God.

We know that the whole creation has been groaning as in the pains of childbirth right up to the present time. (Rom. 8:20–22)

The apostle Paul says that creation has been "groaning" ever since Genesis 3. According to Paul, creation will continue to run down, deteriorate, and decay. We must be good stewards of the planet God has entrusted to us, but the truth is that all of our pollution controls and recycling efforts will not stop the downward spiral of our fallen planet. But God is in control and has a plan. There is coming a day when creation will be liberated from sin and disease, and God will bring a New Heaven and a New Earth.

We currently live in a world that has been permanently scarred by sin. But to fully grasp our future Heaven, it's critical that we see the parallels between God's original place for mankind and His future home for us.

As we walk through what the Bible actually says about Heaven, here is a visual to give you a comprehensive overview of God's passion to be with His people.

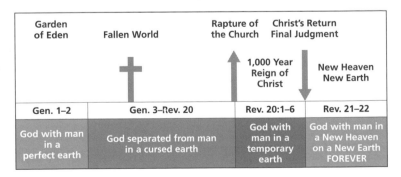

We know that what happens throughout the rest of the Bible is God's redemptive story. We see Old Testament law and sacrifices. We find prophets declaring the truth of God. Finally the Messiah comes in the person of Jesus. He lives a perfect life and makes the ultimate sacrifice by dying on the cross for our sins. Three days later He rises from the dead and then later ascends back into Heaven. Then the Holy Spirit comes at Pentecost and the church is born. And the church is given the task of the Great Commission—going into all the earth to share the good news of the gospel. And this period of time called the church age is the age in which we are living right now.

> **To fully grasp our future Heaven, it's critical that we see the parallels between God's original place for mankind and His future home for us.**

But there is coming a day when Jesus will come and He will take the church from the earth. That event is commonly referred to as *the rapture*. That "snatching away" of Christians off the earth is followed by seven years of tribulation, and that seven-year period culminates with Jesus returning to earth in judgment. And for a thousand years Jesus will be judge and king on this earth. At the end of that thousand years there will be the Great White Throne judgment, which is the judgment and sentencing of unbelievers. Following that final judgment, the New Heaven and the New Earth arrive on the scene.

I don't know about you, but when I was growing up, I never heard about a New Heaven or a New Earth. For so many of us, it is hard to mentally grasp what Heaven is like, because most of us have grown up picturing Heaven like I mentioned earlier—people floating on clouds in white robes playing harps. That image is bizarre and vague and was created by Hollywood. So, while I don't have experience with floating around on clouds and I've never even picked up a harp, I do have a lot of years experiencing this earth. I've seen mountains and lakes and oceans and rivers. I've witnessed amazing sunsets that fill me with wonder and awe. I've experienced culture and beauty and music. I know what it is to discover and to have adventure. And it isn't hard at all to imagine a Heaven that is similar to this earth . . . only infinitely better.

Let's suppose for a moment that you are driving around in a ten-year-old car. The paint is chipped and the upholstery is showing some wear and tear and the car has a hard time starting in the cold. And let's imagine that I come to you and offer you a brand-new car. I don't think you would say, "I have no idea what a new car is like." You know what a car is and you know that this new car will have similarities to your old car. And you also know that it will be better. It will get better gas mileage, it will be more comfortable, it will drive better, and the upholstery won't be stained and torn. That is the New Heaven and the New Earth. The New Heaven has similar characteristics and qualities as the old earth, but infinitely better.

The Heaven that God has planned for you is very much like the paradise He created in the beginning for Adam and Eve. There was perfect relationship and life and beauty and work and discovery and enjoyment. It was real life with real people on a real earth. And that is what awaits us in our future.

God promises that in the future, Heaven will literally come down, and there be a New Heaven (called the New Jerusalem) on a New Earth, with none of the problems of this fallen earth.

The Heaven we will encounter will mirror some of our most treasured moments that feel like Heaven on earth. Recently, I had one of those experiences that only a grandpa can appreciate. One of my grandsons spent the night with us, and the next morning I took him to school. As I was walking away after dropping him off, he ran down the hall and grabbed my leg. Then he grabbed my arm and pulled me down to where he could look me in the eye. He hugged me real tight and then said, "I love you, Poppaw." He went a few steps toward his classroom and then turned around and waved at me

The Heaven that God has planned for you is very much like the paradise He created in the beginning for Adam and Eve.

again. Then just as he was about to go into his classroom, he turned around one more time and yelled out, "Poppaw!" and waved again. It was pure, unadulterated love, and it doesn't get any better than that. That, my friend, is just a taste of what God has in store for us.

Maybe you remember the first time you held your child and the emotion you felt. And you remember that overwhelming feeling of absolute joy and wonder. The awe that you experienced in that moment is a sampling of what we will experience in the New Heaven and the New Earth.

Some of us have experienced the deep satisfaction of a marriage that is incredibly fulfilling and intimate. You have done life with a person who knows everything about you and still loves and accepts you unconditionally. To have a mate who believes in you, encourages you, respects you, loves you, and stands by you when everybody else has left . . . that is a gift. You can't imagine life without them. You didn't think you could ever love anyone like that, and you didn't think anyone would ever love you like that. And that, my friend, is a small preview of what is coming. As good as that experience is, it is the "ten-year-old car" compared to the new car God is preparing for you.

The best that you have known and experienced and felt on this earth is but a pale glimmer of what God has planned for us in the New Heaven and the New Earth.

In fact, let's go ahead and see how John describes the New Heaven and the New Earth in Revelation 21. Remember that he is describing a real place. It has similarities to this earth, but it exceeds our wildest dreams.

Then I saw "a new heaven and a new earth," for the first heaven and the first earth had passed away, and there was no longer any sea. I saw the Holy City, the New Jerusalem, coming down out of heaven from God, prepared as a bride beautifully dressed for her husband. And I heard a loud voice from the throne saying, "Look! God's dwelling place is now among the people, and he will dwell with them. They will be his people, and God himself will be with them and be their God. 'He will wipe every tear from their eyes. There will be no more death' or mourning or crying or pain, for the old order of things has passed away."

He who was seated on the throne said, "I am making everything new!" Then he said, "Write this down, for these words are trustworthy and true." (vv. 1–5)

God is going to make "everything new." The word "new" isn't a reference to new in time or chronology. Rather, this word refers to new in quality or character. It is new in the sense that it is qualitatively an upgrade to the old earth.

And like the old earth, there will be nations and cities and art and music and beauty and relationships. Stop for a moment! Have you ever thought about Heaven like that? Do you see why Paul was eager to depart?

> **The best that you have known and experienced and felt on this earth is but a pale glimmer of what God has planned for us in the New Heaven and the New Earth.**

As you let that soak in, let me conclude this chapter by going back to where we started. God wants to be with you. Notice verse 3 of Revelation 21. It is highly relational, as John announces that God's dwelling place is now with His people. Two different times in that one verse John declares that God will be "with" us. He longs for you to come home and He has carefully crafted a place and an environment that will be beyond your wildest dreams. The real essence of Heaven is about more than just a place, it is about a person. It is about coming home to our heavenly Father who loves ordinary people like you and me the same way He loves Jesus.

4

WHAT *REALLY* HAPPENS AFTER I DIE?

Therefore we are always confident and know that as long as we are at home in the body we are away from the Lord. For we live by faith, not by sight. We are confident, I say, and would prefer to be away from the body and at home with the Lord.

2 Corinthians 5:6–8

I want you to imagine that it is a typical Sunday morning. You and your family have made your way to church. By the time you get there, the service has already started but you are able to find seats in the section where you normally sit. After a few minutes of singing worship songs, your pastor steps to the podium, but instead of starting a normal sermon, he lets you know he wants to take an informal survey of the congregation.

This is not anything new in your church. Occasionally the pastor will take a survey just to get the pulse of the congregation on a particular subject. But the question he asks the congregation today catches you a bit off guard. He asks, "If you were given the choice of going to Heaven today or waiting ten years, how many of you would choose waiting the ten years?"

Honestly, it's a question you have never considered before. But as you look around the auditorium, the majority of people have raised their hands. So, how about you? Which would you choose . . . go to Heaven today or wait ten more years?

I am confident that if your congregation were asked that question next Sunday, the overwhelming majority would choose to wait ten years. Even though this world isn't perfect, most of us generally like our lives here in this world. And we dream of things we still want to do and we still want time to enjoy family and friends. And life here is mostly comfortable and familiar and known. But there is so much about Heaven that is unknown and a little unsettling.

It is interesting that people in Scripture, like the apostle Paul, longed for Heaven in ways that we don't. And I have to be honest and tell you that, until the last few years, I didn't give Heaven much thought, much less long to go there. However, I started thinking about Heaven a lot when my wife, Theresa, got cancer. She has totally recovered, but the journey we went through forced me, like never before, to contemplate our mortality. In the last several years we have buried my parents and Theresa's mom, and as a result, I've begun to think a lot more about Heaven.

The older I get, I realize I'm not going to be around too many more years, and I think more about eternity and Heaven. The more I have dug into this material, the deeper my conviction has become that Heaven is REAL and it is better. Certainly God has given us some great gifts in this life and on this planet. We know what it is to experience joy and beauty and love and purpose. But the best that we have known and experienced in this life is but the appetizer for the main entrée that is to come in Heaven. The more I grasp what God has prepared for me, the more I feel the grip of this world being loosened and the more I begin to feel a longing for Heaven.

> **The best that we have known and experienced in this life is but the appetizer for the main entrée that is to come in Heaven.**

In the last chapter, we talked about God's original Heaven on earth called the Garden of Eden. And we spent some time talking about the New Heaven and the New Earth that is still to come in the future. But what does the Bible say about the Christian who dies during that time between Genesis 3 and Revelation 20? What happens to them? Answering that question clearly will help loosen the grip of this world on us and stir in us a deeper desire for Heaven.

The Bible is clear that when Christians die, they immediately go into the presence of God. That is often referred to by scholars and theologians as the Intermediate Heaven. That is not a phrase you will find in the Bible but is simply used to differentiate where Christians go now when they die as opposed to the New Heaven and the New Earth, which is to come later.

The last two chapters of Revelation usher in a new chapter in God's plan. In Revelation 21 and 22 we see the unveiling of the New Heaven and the New Earth. And we will live in this New Heaven and New Earth in resurrected bodies.

Knowing the final outcome and destination brings great comfort and anticipation; but a question I'm often asked when I teach on the Intermediate Heaven and the New Heaven is this:

> As a follower of Jesus, what would happen one minute after you die? If you had a massive heart attack today and took your last breath on this earth, what does the Bible tell us would happen to you in that next moment?

1. Angels will usher your soul to Heaven.

> The time came when the beggar died and the angels carried him to Abraham's side. The rich man also died and was buried.
>
> Luke 16:22

In Luke 16 Jesus tells a story of a rich man and a poor beggar named Lazarus. The point of this compelling story is not to teach us about Heaven, but nonetheless we can learn some valuable insight about Heaven from it. In the story the rich man lived a life of luxurious excess and Lazarus lived in abject poverty. Eventually both men die and Lazarus goes to Abraham's side, which represents where the righteous go when they die. The rich man, on the other hand, finds himself in Hades, a place of torment.

Actually, verse 22 of Luke 16 says that when Lazarus died, the "angels carried him to Abraham's side."

That last line reminds me of a great story that comes out of the missionary efforts to reach the Auca Indians. Also known as the Huaorani, this Ecuadorian tribe was one of the fiercest in all of South America. There were five missionaries that were working together to share the gospel with the Huaorani people. They used their airplane to first make contact by using a loudspeaker and a basket to lower down gifts. A few months later they decided to build a base near the Indian village along the river. The missionaries had a couple of friendly encounters with people from the tribe. So the missionaries were making plans to journey to the village to make further contact in hopes of eventually being able to share the gospel. However, before they could make their journey, ten Huaorani warriors attacked them at their base camp, and all five missionaries were martyred. The two most well-known of those missionaries were Jim Elliot and Nate Saint.

After these missionaries were killed, their wives banded together and decided they would continue the work of their martyred husbands and carry the gospel to the Auca people. Miraculously, through their efforts, many of the Hauorani tribe came to faith in Christ. Some of the warriors who were converted to Christ recounted that infamous day when they murdered those five missionaries. The warriors said that after they killed them, there was singing in the trees. And figures clothed in white hovered over the bodies and carried them to the sky.

Amazing as it sounds, our heavenly Father so much wants to be with you that the moment you die, He is going to make sure you are immediately escorted to Heaven.

2. Heaven becomes your forever home.

In the same story in Luke 16 of the rich man and Lazarus, we also learn something else about Heaven. The rich man looked up from Hades and saw Abraham, with Lazarus sitting by his side. The rich man cries out to Abraham to have Lazarus come and dip the tip of his finger in water so that he might cool the tongue of the rich man in Hades.

> **In other words, once you die, your eternal destiny is set. Your future is secure.**

In verse 26, Abraham responds by saying, *"Between us and you a great chasm has been set in place, so that those who want to go from here to you cannot, nor can anyone cross over from there to us."*

In other words, once you die, your eternal destiny is set. Your future is secure. No one can cross over the great chasm that Abraham referred to. And no one who is in Heaven will ever have to worry about losing their place or home in Heaven.

3. You immediately enter God's presence.

The apostle Paul says,

> Therefore we are always confident and know that as long as
> we are at home in the body we are away from the Lord. For we
> live by faith, not by sight. We are confident, I say, and would
> prefer to be away from the body and at home with the Lord.
> (2 Cor. 5:6–8)

To be away from the body is to be at home with the Lord. One minute after you die, you will be in the presence of God. In the moment your soul departs your body, you will be in His presence. There is no delay. There is no purgatory. There is no reincarnation.

At the moment a Christian takes their last breath, they are immediately in the presence of Christ.

At the height of his professional career, the great golfer Paul Azinger was given the news that he had life-threatening cancer. "That encounter with the inevitability of eternity was

"We think that we are in the land of the living going to the land of the dying when in reality we are in the land of the dying headed for the land of the living."

an abrupt reality check. His life would never be the same. . . . All he could think about was what the chaplain of the golf tour had said: 'We think that we are in the land of the living going to the land of the dying when in reality we are in the land of the dying headed for the land of the living.'"[5]

From the earthly side, we feel the sting of death. We see an ashen corpse and a sterile casket. We emotionally experience loss and sorrow. But if we could see this experience from the heavenly side, we would see a quite different scene. We would see a spirit that is more alive than it has ever been. We would emotionally experience the joy and gladness of someone who has come home.

There is an intriguing story from the life of Winston Churchill that illustrates both the earthly and heavenly perspectives of Heaven:

> The British Prime Minister, as he was making plans for his funeral, asked to be laid in state in the heart of London at St. Paul's Cathedral. He requested that his casket be placed under the massive dome in the center of the Cathedral. Churchill then requested two trumpeters be stationed on each side of that balcony that circles the dome. It was his wish that at the close of the service the trumpeter on one side would play taps. When he was finished the trumpeter on the other side was to play reveille.[6]

Taps would represent the closing of life on this planet, and reveille would represent the wake-up call to a new life in Heaven.

This life is a journey of winding turns. We cannot always see where the road is leading, but we know the final destination. There is no question whether or not we will make it or if it will be good when we get there. We literally will live happily ever after. We are going home. Every morning when you awake, you can tell yourself, "I am one day closer to home."

It is important to understand that upon your death your spirit is immediately in the presence of Christ, but you won't have a resurrected body yet. That will come later.

But the real you is your soul. The body is simply the container that houses your soul. Your body will age and deteriorate and become diseased and eventually die, but that will never happen to your soul. Our souls live in this Intermediate Heaven in the presence of God until Revelation 21 and 22 when the New Heaven and the New Earth arrive.

At the core of our faith is the belief that you have been given one life. Hebrews says that *"it is appointed unto men once to die, but after this the judgment"* (9:27 KJV). Your eternal destiny is determined by the decision you make in this life. It is in this one life that you make the decision to either receive or reject Jesus Christ. For those who have received Jesus Christ as their Savior, the moment they die they are ushered into Heaven into the presence of God.

> **We literally will live happily ever after. We are going home.**

4. You are conscious and in command of your faculties of thought, feelings, speech, and memories.

Again, the story of the rich man and Lazarus in Luke 16 is very helpful in understanding this issue.

This passage can raise a lot of questions, but what is clear is that people in the afterlife function very much like we do here in this life. They have emotions and feelings. People are able to have conversation and dialogue with one another. They are conscious and even aware of their past. And even though people do not have a resurrected body at this point, they still possess all the qualities of personality and personhood. This is important, because it helps us understand that our personhood doesn't come from our body. It comes from our soul—the "real you."

I could get in my car today and be in an accident. And as a result they might have to amputate my arm. That doesn't change who I am. I am still Chip. You could have an organ transplant and it wouldn't fundamentally change who you are. You aren't a different person because you have a different kidney. Your identity is not defined by a body part. It is your soul that defines you and houses all the traits of your personality.

When you die, your soul (the real you) will continue to be able to function by thinking, feeling, dialoguing, knowing, and being aware.

How does this all work? What will we experience or not experience with regard to time? How much will we be aware of what's happening on the earth? These are all great questions that remain a mystery. We can make inferences and educated guesses, but what we learn for certain is that we will be in the presence of God.

5

WHAT WILL WE *REALLY* DO IN THE INTERMEDIATE HEAVEN?

Then I heard every creature in heaven and on earth and under the earth and on the sea, and all that is in them, saying: "To him who sits on the throne and to the Lamb be praise and honor and glory and power, for ever and ever!"

Revelation 5:13

Although we don't have lots of details, and there is certainly much we don't know, there are some things that we know for sure. When we die and arrive at the Intermediate Heaven, the Scripture describes three things we will do.

1. You participate in magnificent worship with angels and believers before the throne of God and Christ.

In the book of Revelation Jesus gives the apostle John the privilege of getting a glimpse of Heaven. Jesus pulls back the veil just a little bit and allows John to actually see what happens in the afterlife for those who are Christ-followers. Let me remind you again, this is not a picture of the New Heaven and the New Earth, but it is a picture of what is going on now in the Intermediate Heaven.

There are two very important things to understand about what is taking place in Revelation 4. First, this is actually happening right now as you read these words. Right now, in this moment, thousands upon thousands are participating in worship of Almighty God. If you have a friend or loved one who was a Christ-follower but has died, this is what they are experiencing right now. And remember, they are conscious, they have emotion, and they are able to have conversation. They are still Bill, or Ann, or Frank, or Stephanie. Their personhood has not been eliminated or diminished in any way. Second, this is not what Heaven is like forever. Years ago when I first read this passage, I thought that this was the description of what was going to happen for all of eternity. What I have since discovered is that what happens here is magnificent, it is amazing, it is mind-blowing . . . but it is not the whole picture.

So, let's take a glimpse at this snapshot of the most amazing worship service ever:

> After this I looked, and there before me was a door standing open in heaven. And the voice I had first heard speaking to

me like a trumpet said, "Come up here, and I will show you what must take place after this." At once I was in the Spirit, and there before me was a throne in heaven with someone sitting on it. And the one who sat there had the appearance of jasper and ruby. A rainbow that shone like an emerald encircled the throne. Surrounding the throne were twenty-four other thrones, and seated on them were twenty-four elders. They were dressed in white and had crowns of gold on their heads. From the throne came flashes of lightning, rumblings and peals of thunder. In front of the throne, seven lamps were blazing. (Rev. 4:1–6)

Did you notice how many times the word "throne" is used in this passage? What do people do from thrones? They rule! In this glimpse of Heaven, it becomes very clear that there is someone in charge and in control.

There is only one throne in Heaven and it is a single seater. We will be worshiping around that throne and everything about us will be aligned with His Lordship. So, let me ask you, How are you doing in this life regarding submission to that throne? What God has revealed about Heaven is meant not only for hope and comfort but as an example to learn from and follow.

> **What God has revealed about Heaven is meant not only for hope and comfort but as an example to learn from and follow.**

Surrounding the throne are these four living creatures, and day and night they continually say, "'*Holy, holy, holy is the Lord*

God Almighty,' who was, and is, and is to come" (Rev. 4:8). In Heaven the worship is focused on God and His character. He is *holy*. The word means to be "set apart" or "wholly other." There is none like Him. He is not like us. He is not just a better "you." There is no category to place Him in. He is perfect and righteous and without sin. And He is worthy of our worship and praise.

He is also all-powerful. In Daniel 4:34–35 Nebuchadnezzar speaks of God's power when he says:

> Then I praised the Most High; I honored and glorified him who lives forever.
>
> His dominion is an eternal dominion;
>> his kingdom endures from generation to generation.
> All the peoples of the earth
>> are regarded as nothing.
> He does as he pleases
>> with the powers of heaven
>> and the peoples of the earth.
> No one can hold back his hand
>> or say to him: "What have you done?"

He does exactly as He pleases and no one is able to stop Him or hinder Him from completing His purposes.

And these four living creatures in Revelation 4 also exalt the fact that God is eternal. These creatures talk about God "who was." He existed in eternity past and there was never a time He didn't exist. They also declare that God "is," which means He is present in the "now." He is not a disinterested third party; He is alive and present and engaged in today. And He is the God who is "to come." There is no moment out in the future when He ceases to exist. He is forever and ever. He is the uncreated One, the infinite reference point. He is the center and focal point for all of life past, present, and future.

This magnificent worship service continues on into chapter 5 of Revelation. John says there was a Lamb, looking as if it had been slain, standing at the center of the throne. Four living creatures and twenty-four elders surrounded the throne, fell down in worship, and began to sing.

It is always interesting to see how people in the Bible respond to the majesty and holiness of God. Occasionally I will meet people who talk about going to Heaven and they can't wait to run up and jump in God's lap. That notion is certainly very different than what happens in the Bible when people encounter God in all of His glory.

In Isaiah 6, Isaiah says that he saw the Lord high and lifted up. In verse 5 of that chapter, Isaiah's response was to say, *"Woe to me! . . . I am ruined. I am a man of unclean lips."* Isaiah's response was to declare his unworthiness and brokenness. The light of God's glory caused Isaiah to see the darkness of his own sin.

In the first chapter of Revelation, the apostle John has a vision of Christ in all of His majesty. John sees something that is supernatural, something (actually Someone) that defies description. Yet he tries to find words to describe what he witnesses. He says His eyes were *like* blazing fire and His feet were *like* bronze glowing in a furnace. He says that His voice was *like* the sound of rushing waters and His face was *like* the sun shining in all its brilliance.

When John witnesses this incredible scene, he says, *"When I saw him, I fell at his feet as though dead"* (Rev. 1:17).

There wasn't any running up to Jesus and climbing in His lap. When people encounter the all-knowing, all-powerful, holy, and infinite God of time and eternity, they are so overcome with His glory and majesty that all they can do is fall down in worship. That's exactly what the four living creatures and twenty-four elders do in Revelation 5.

But they don't just fall down, they begin to sing a song of worship . . .

And they sang a new song, saying:

"You are worthy to take the scroll
    and to open its seals,
because you were slain,
    and with your blood you purchased for God
    persons from every tribe and language and people
    and nation.
You have made them to be a kingdom and priests to
    serve our God,
    and they will reign on the earth." (Rev. 5:9–10)

When we go to Heaven, we will have an acute understanding of what our salvation cost, and that will make our worship that much richer. We will sometimes see angels engaged in worship. That is part of their role and purpose. But there is one huge difference between our worship and the angels' worship. We understand grace and redemption in a way that angels never can. We know what it is to be desperately broken and then to be pursued by God. We know what it is like to have Jesus love us enough to die for our sin. We know what it is to sing the words "Once I was lost, but now I am found."

> **When people encounter the all-knowing, all-powerful, holy, and infinite God of time and eternity, they are so overcome with His glory and majesty that all they can do is fall down in worship.**

From this passage in Revelation 5, I also want you to notice the last phrase of verse 10, "they will reign on the earth." Their reigning on earth is in the future. What we are witnessing here in Revelation 5 is a worship service. In fact, it is not a stretch to say that this is the mother of all worship services.

And the participation isn't limited to these four living creatures and the elders around the throne. Verse 11 says that the angels join in as well. And not just a few:

> Then I looked and heard the voice of many angels, numbering thousands upon thousands, and ten thousand times ten thousand. They encircled the throne and the living creatures and the elders. In a loud voice they were saying:

"Worthy is the Lamb, who was slain,
to receive power and wealth and wisdom and strength
and honor and glory and praise!" (vv. 11–12)

And it's not just limited to the four living creatures and the elders and the angels. In verse 13 John says that "every creature" joins in:

Then I heard every creature in heaven and on earth and under the earth and on the sea, and all that is in them, saying:

"To him who sits on the throne and to the Lamb
be praise and honor and glory and power,
for ever and ever!"

What a contrast to some of the worship services in our churches. In Heaven no one is sitting passively with folded arms. No one is scrolling through their emails on their smartphone. No one is bored and disinterested. There is full-on singing and praise and adoration and honor for the living God who was, and is, and is to come.

As wonderful as joining this worship service will be, it's not the only thing one will experience in the Intermediate Heaven.

2. You are aware to some degree of activities and events on earth.

There has always been a lot of discussion and speculation about what level of awareness people in Heaven will have about activities on the earth. Revelation 6 provides us some insight into this issue.

> When he opened the fifth seal, I saw under the altar the souls of those who had been slain because of the word of God and the testimony they had maintained. They called out in a loud voice, "How long, Sovereign Lord, holy and true, until you judge the inhabitants of the earth and avenge our blood?" Then each of them was given a white robe, and they were told to wait a little longer, until the full number of their fellow servants, their brothers and sisters, were killed just as they had been. (vv. 9–11)

John says that under the altar in Heaven are the "souls of those who had been slain." The word "soul" is actually the Greek word *psuché*. We get our words "psyche" and "psychology" from this ancient Greek word. Sometimes the word "soul" can refer to the immaterial, nonphysical part of us. But, at other times, the word is used to describe the entire person.

In Heaven no one is sitting passively with folded arms. No one is scrolling through their emails on their smartphone. No one is bored and disinterested.

The soul is the unseen, eternal you. It is the "real" you. Someday your body is going to wear out and you are going to take your last breath and your heart is going to beat for the last time. They are going to pronounce you dead and have a funeral for you. But we Christians, above all people, know that is not the end of you. So, if you are a Christ-follower, even when they pronounce you dead, your soul (the real you) will be alive and well. And your earthly death is simply your soul's transition into Heaven.

In verse 10 of Revelation 6, these people (souls) call out to God and ask how long it will be before He judges the inhabitants of the earth and avenges their deaths. The very question implies some level of knowledge regarding what is happening on the earth. I've read and heard many sermons that depict our loved ones being aware of all our actions. I've heard star athletes talk about their mom or dad watching their game and that he or she is doing their best for them. The Bible is not specific. Some level of awareness seems clear, but just how much is unknown.

> **The very question in Revelation 6:10 implies some level of knowledge regarding what is happening on the earth.**

But whether it is little or much, have you noticed that we all behave a little differently when we know someone is watching us? Have you ever been walking or jogging down the street and then a car turns the corner and starts toward you? I suspect that you do just what I do. I start to jog faster until the car passes.

When I was a teenager and in high school, I really looked up to my sister, Punkie. She was an amazing person and had a significant influence on my life. She was only about a year and four months older than me, but she was my hero. She took great interest in my life and we even took a couple of classes together in high school. She was the nicest, kindest person I had known. And she really believed in me and thought more highly of me than I deserved. It's hard to articulate, but something deep inside me wanted to live up to her expectations and beliefs about me. At the time, I wasn't aware that she was a Christian. Later I would discover she had become a Christ-follower in her sophomore year.

There were multiple occasions in high school when I would be at a party and there would be a lot of alcohol, marijuana, and uppers. As I was confronted with that temptation, the thing that restrained me wasn't fear of my parents finding out or concern as an athlete that I would mess up my body. In those moments of temptation, the picture I had in my mind was that of my sister. I could envision the disappointment in her eyes and could hear her say, "Chip, I can't believe you would do that."

It could be that your mom or grandparent or friend who is in Heaven has some awareness of what we do here. If our view of Heaven was less about clouds and harps and more about real people that we care about who have some awareness of life on earth, it might just change our behavior . . . just like my desire to not disappoint my sister kept me from certain behaviors in high school.

> **If our view of Heaven was less about clouds and harps and more about real people that we care about who have some awareness of life on earth, it might just change our behavior.**

I can't tell you definitively how much your loved ones in Heaven see or don't see, but it's obvious they have some level of awareness. And even if they don't, knowing God sees all things at all times is plenty of motivation for me.

The third thing you'll do in the Intermediate Heaven is have a few "mini-reunions."

3. You will recognize and communicate with believers who preceded you to Heaven.

Luke records for us this amazing experience called the Transfiguration. Peter, James, and John get a front-row seat to an unbelievable supernatural experience. In this moment, it is as if the veil of Jesus' humanity is pulled back and these three disciples get a glimpse into the deity and glory of Jesus. They not only see Jesus glorified, but Moses and Elijah also appear.

About eight days after Jesus said this, he took Peter, John and James with him and went up onto a mountain to pray. As he was praying, the appearance of his face changed, and his clothes became as bright as a flash of lightning. Two men, Moses and Elijah, appeared in glorious splendor, talking with Jesus. They spoke about his departure, which he was about to bring to fulfillment at Jerusalem. Peter and his companions were very sleepy, but when they became fully awake, they saw his glory and the two men standing with him. As the men were leaving Jesus, Peter said to him, "Master, it is good for us to be here. Let us put up three shelters—one for you, one for Moses and one for Elijah." (He did not know what he was saying.)

While he was speaking, a cloud appeared and covered them, and they were afraid as they entered the cloud. A voice came from the cloud, saying, "This is my Son, whom I have chosen; listen to him." When the voice had spoken, they found that Jesus was alone. The disciples kept this to themselves and did not tell anyone at that time what they had seen. (Luke 9:28–36)

We are not quite sure how it happened, but Peter was able to recognize Moses and Elijah. Verse 30 says that Moses and Elijah appeared in glorious splendor. There was obviously a transformation that had happened to these two great men. They were obviously not in the same body they had when they lived on earth hundreds of years earlier. But they were still the same people . . . Moses and Elijah.

Notice also in the passage that Jesus has a conversation with Moses and Elijah that day on the mountaintop. The Bible even tells us what they talk about. They dialogued about the impending departure of Jesus.

This truth gives me great hope about what I will experience moments after I die and what those I love will experience as followers of Jesus. While I was working on this material, a very good friend of mine lost someone very close to him. After pondering and studying what happens in the Intermediate Heaven, I could relate to him the hope and future of his friend like never before.

Losing people you love is hard and painful, and we grieve being separated from those we care about so deeply. But the hope and assurance of the Bible is that this life is not all there is. There is a real place where you will be reunited with Christians who have died before you. You will recognize and talk with your loved ones and heroes of the faith in the Intermediate Heaven.

And while it doesn't do away with the sorrow and grief that we feel in this life, it tempers it with the reality that the separation is only temporary.

As we wrap up this chapter, let's go back to where we started. You have had a massive heart attack and they have pronounced you dead. What happens in that next minute?

- God sends His angels to usher you into the presence of God.

- You are conscious and aware of what is happening.

- You are fully alive and fully you. You just don't have a glorified body at this point.

- You are conscious and at least somewhat aware of what is happening on the earth.

- You will recognize and be reunited with believers who preceded you to Heaven.

And then you see this massive throne and surrounding that throne are angels and elders and these living creatures. And you see Jesus and He is holy and majestic and powerful and wise. You realize you are now in the presence of the one and only God. You are standing before the One who is the sovereign ruler of everything. You have never witnessed anything so beautiful in all your life. You are immediately overwhelmed by this magnificent worship service taking place.

That is what Heaven is like. And we are just getting started.

6

HOW WILL HUMAN HISTORY *REALLY* END?

PART 1

For the Lord himself will come down from heaven, with a loud command, with the voice of the archangel and with the trumpet call of God, and the dead in Christ will rise first. After that, we who are still alive and are left will be caught up together with them in the clouds to meet the Lord in the air. And so we will be with the Lord forever.

1 Thessalonians 4:16–17

Humans have always been intrigued with the future. There is something in us that wants to know what is coming. When I have discussions with people about the authority and credibility of the Bible, I will often talk about the Messianic prophecies made in the Old Testament. More than 300 prophecies about the future coming of the Messiah are found throughout the Old Testament. Hundreds of years in advance, prophets talked about where He would be born, the lineage He would come from, how He would die, and even where He would be buried. With incredible precision and accuracy, God foretold the future through these prophets. So when the Bible speaks about the future, there is good reason for us to pay attention.

The Bible not only foretold the first coming of Jesus to earth, but it has a lot to say about His return and the future events surrounding His return.

As people living in the twenty-first century, what can we know about the future? What does the Bible say about the final chapters of human history? Well, the good news is that God has spoken and has revealed the key events that will take place in the future. Let's take a look at some of those significant events.

1. Jesus will "rapture" the church from the earth.

Sometimes when we pick up our Bible, we think of it as individual books with chapters and verses. But it is helpful for us to occasionally remind ourselves that the sixty-six books of the Bible make up one book. And it is one story. It is God's story.

Let's take just a few moments to get a big-picture view of the story that God is writing.

In Genesis 1 and 2 God creates a perfect environment called the Garden of Eden. In Genesis 3 sin enters the world and Adam and Eve are exiled from the garden. That is followed by the rest of the Old Testament with all of the history of Israel and all of the ups and downs of them following God and then falling into rebellion and sin. In the Old Testament we also have the prophets who declare the truth of God and also point to a future day when God would provide a Messiah who would pay for their sin.

> The sixty-six books of the Bible make up one book. And it is one story. It is God's story.

When we get to the New Testament, Jesus comes to earth, born of a virgin (fully God and fully man), lives a perfect sinless life, and after thirty-three years, dies on the cross. Three days later He rises from the dead, and then after several appearances to over five hundred witnesses, He ascends back into Heaven. Jesus' final words were a command to make disciples of all nations and a promise of His continued presence through the Holy Spirit. Then you come to the book of Acts and the event of Pentecost when the Holy Spirit comes to indwell all believers.

Because of Israel's continued disobedience and rebellion, God temporarily sets them aside as His agent of blessing after they reject their King and Messiah, Jesus. It is somewhat like a coach who calls a time-out and takes a player who isn't playing well and puts them on the bench. They're not off the team (God will fulfill all the promises to Israel one day); they will play again. But, for right now, they sit on the bench and the coach puts in a new player.

Well, when you come to the book of Acts, the new player that God puts in is called the church. The church is a supernatural community of Jews and Gentiles who have been spiritually born again. Starting in the book of Acts we have what is commonly referred to as the "church age." And that is the age in God's plan we are now living in.

The next event in the story that God is writing is called the *rapture*. Now, you won't find the word "rapture" in the Bible, but the truth and teaching is there. You also won't find the word "trinity" in the Bible, but it is a word that portrays a Biblical reality of the triune Godhead. The same is true with the word "rapture." The word simply means "to snatch," and the idea is that Jesus will come and rapture (snatch away) all believers living on the earth and take them to Heaven. And the rapture could happen at any moment.

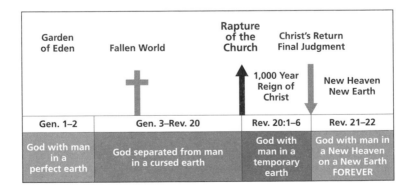

This event is best described in 1 Thessalonians 4:13–18:

> Brothers and sisters, we do not want you to be uninformed about those who sleep in death, so that you do not grieve like the rest of mankind, who have no hope. For we believe that Jesus died and rose again, and so we believe that God will bring with Jesus those who have fallen asleep in him. According to the Lord's word, we tell you that we who are still alive, who are left until the coming of the Lord, will certainly not precede those who have fallen asleep. For the Lord himself will come down from heaven, with a loud command, with the voice of the archangel and with the trumpet call of God, and the dead in Christ will rise first. After that, we who are still alive and are left will be caught up together with them in the clouds to meet the Lord in the air. And so we will be with the Lord forever. Therefore encourage one another with these words.

At the rapture, every Christian is taken off the earth and immediately transported to Heaven. You will notice in the passage that Paul says just prior to believers being raptured off the earth, the dead in Christ will rise first. Their spirits have already gone to be with the Lord in Heaven. But now, at the rapture, their bodies will be resurrected and they will be given a glorified body. And the clear implication is that those believers who are alive and raptured will be given new glorified bodies as they are taken into Heaven.

Paul describes this event in 1 Corinthians 15:51–53:

> Listen, I tell you a mystery: We will not all sleep, but we will all be changed—in a flash, in the twinkling of an eye, at the

last trumpet. For the trumpet will sound, the dead will be raised imperishable, and we will be changed. For the perishable must clothe itself with the imperishable, and the mortal with immortality.

When Paul talks about this being a mystery, he is not talking about something that is hard to understand. Rather, a *mystery* in Scripture is something that was hidden in the past and is now revealed. The mystery of the rapture was not revealed to Old Testament saints but is now revealed in the New Testament.

We can also deduce from this passage that the rapture could happen at any moment. There are no other signs that have to be fulfilled before Jesus could come in the clouds and rapture His church off the earth.

You will also notice that in verse 52 Paul says at the rapture we will be "changed." Christians who had already died will receive their glorified bodies in the rapture. And Christians who are alive at the time of the rapture will also receive their glorified bodies. Their natural bodies, marred by sin and disease, are not fit for Heaven. They will trade in their temporal bodies for eternal ones. They will exchange their imperfect bodies for perfect bodies.

A few verses earlier Paul talked specifically about the glorified bodies we will receive at the rapture. He says,

When you sow, you do not plant the body that will be, but just a seed, perhaps of wheat or of something else. But God gives it a body as he has determined, and to each kind of seed he gives its own body. (1 Cor. 15:37–38)

Paul's illustration is simple and clear. When you plant a seed of wheat or corn, what eventually comes out of the ground is very different from the seed. There is continuity, but there is also a glorious and noticeable difference. The same will be true of our glorified bodies. They will come from the seed of our human bodies . . . so there will be continuity. But they will be exponentially better and more glorious.

In verse 42 of 1 Corinthians 15, Paul says, *"So will it be with the resurrection of the dead. The body that is sown is perishable, it is raised imperishable."*

Think about this for just a moment. The body you now have is perishable. When you go to the grocery store and buy a perishable item, it means it has an expiration date. It won't last forever. It has a certain shelf life. The same is true with your physical, earthly body. It has an expiration date. And the older we get, the more we become acutely aware that our body is perishable. It begins to break down, slow down, and wear down. But thank God our glorified body will be imperishable. There will be no expiration date. It will never get old or diseased. It will be the ultimate upgrade.

> **Thank God our glorified body will be imperishable. There will be no expiration date. It will never get old or diseased. It will be the ultimate upgrade.**

2. There will be tribulation on the earth and celebration in Heaven.

After the rapture, a seven-year terrible period of time begins that is called the tribulation. The events of the tribulation are described in Revelation 6–20. The first three and a half years of the tribulation are peaceful. During this time there is one leader over the entire earth who ends up deluding people. We know him as the Antichrist, and the Bible says that he is energized by Satan. And then in the last three and a half years of the tribulation, he unleashes his fury on the earth, and there is devastation and judgment like we have never seen before.

While all of this is taking place on the earth, the Bible describes a couple of celebration events that take place in Heaven in which you and I will be honored to participate.

The Judgment Seat of Christ

Now, I admit the word "judgment" may not sound much like a celebration. Usually, the term "judgment" does not fill our heads with warm, fuzzy thoughts. Usually, the word strikes fear in us.

There are many people who grew up fearing the judgment seat of Christ. They believed that when they got to Heaven, their entire life would be shown on a huge heavenly movie screen and everybody in Heaven would watch every secret sin they had committed and every impure thought they ever had. We would only get to enjoy Heaven after we endured the shame and humiliation of this judgment. When you read 2 Corinthians

5:10, you can understand how someone might get that picture in their minds:

> For we must all appear before the judgment seat of Christ, so that each of us may receive what is due us for the things done while in the body, whether good or bad.

But this is not a judgment of shame and humiliation. If you know Christ as your Savior, all your sins have been forgiven and will never be held against you. They will not be on the big screen in Heaven. This is a judgment of *rewards*.

What Paul had in mind when he wrote that verse was the Isthmian games—the forerunner to the Olympics. In this large stadium, the judges presided from a raised platform in the stands called the Bema or "judgment seat." Victorious athletes would ascend the stairs and receive their trophy (which was usually a garland worn around the neck). Also, winners were exempted from taxation for the rest of their lives and their kids could go to school with no cost. The judgment seat of Christ is an awards ceremony, not a time for punishment. It will be about honor, not humiliation. It will not be a time of "shame on you" but rather a time to say "thank you!"

The judgment seat of Christ is an awards ceremony, not a time for punishment.

If it is a judgment of rewards, then what does Paul mean when he says that each "will receive what is due him for the things done, whether good or bad"?

Much misunderstanding comes from this verse. The Greek language has two words for "bad" or "evil" and neither of those words is used here. The word that is used here is the word that means "worthless" or "no lasting value." Paul is saying that when all my motives and deeds are revealed, those that were "worthless" won't receive any kind of reward or commendation. I won't receive punishment or condemnation, but my reward will be less than it might have been.

In our imperfect world, sometimes people get rewarded who don't really deserve the reward. This happens because we can't see everything and often don't know what is going on behind the scenes. This judgment will be absolutely perfect and accurate, because God knows everything and nothing escapes His notice.

> **Those who never heard the cheers of men will hear the cheers of angels. Those who missed the blessing of a father will hear the blessing of their heavenly Father.**

This is a day when God will turn my life inside out. He will not only look at my actions, but the Bible says He will also examine my motives.

There will definitely be some big surprises. Those unknown on earth will be known in Heaven. Those who labored behind the scenes will be heroes in Heaven. Those who never heard the cheers of men will hear the cheers of angels. Those who missed the blessing of a father will hear the blessing of their heavenly Father.

We get more insight into this great event in 1 Corinthians 3:10–15.

By the grace God has given me, I laid a foundation as a wise builder, and someone else is building on it. But each one should build with care. For no one can lay any foundation other than the one already laid, which is Jesus Christ. If anyone builds on this foundation using gold, silver, costly stones, wood, hay or straw, their work will be shown for what it is, because the Day will bring it to light. It will be revealed with fire, and the fire will test the quality of each person's work. If what has been built survives, the builder will receive a reward. If it is burned up, the builder will suffer loss but yet will be saved—even though only as one escaping through the flames.

Paul challenges each one of us to "build with care." Why? Because life is a stewardship. It is a sacred trust. It is not to be taken lightly. Whatever years you have on planet earth were given to you by God. They are a gift. And they were given to you to fulfill God's purposes in your life. And someday He is going to ask for an accounting of what you did with what He gave you. So be careful how you build. Be careful how you spend your 525,600 minutes this year.

In verse 11 Paul talks about the most critical part of any building project—the foundation. He says that there is only one foundation upon which we can really build. That is the foundation of Jesus Christ. The single most important thing you can do to prepare for eternity is to have Jesus Christ as the foundation of your life.

All your plans, all your achievements, all your successes, all your titles—they just don't matter if you have built your life on the wrong foundation.

Paul then speaks about the building materials of life. He says you can use gold, silver, and costly stones or you can use wood, hay, and straw. These materials are representative of your time and your actions. They represent how you spent your life. Did you invest your life for the purposes of God? Did you invest in the things that have eternal value? Were spiritual realities the focus of your time, talents, treasure, and dreams? If so, then you built with gold, silver, and precious stones. Or did you spend all your time pursuing self-interests and temporal, material things?

Obviously, there is a huge qualitative difference between these building materials. Now, this is important because verse 13 says that on the day of this event called the *judgment seat of Christ*, my building project will be tested by fire. Each day and each choice become part of your personal construction project.

> **Each day and each choice become part of your personal construction project.**

Paul says that someday I will present to the Lord the life that I have built. But the Lord will purify it by fire. All of my works will be examined. Those things done out of pride or impure motives will burn like wood, hay, and straw. Whatever is left is what I will be rewarded for.

Paul goes on to say that our "work will be shown for what it is, because the Day will bring it to light." What Day is he referring to? It is the day Paul refers to in Romans 14:10 when he says, *"Remember, each of us will stand personally before the* Judgment Seat of God" (TLB, emphasis added).

I love how one great reformer kept this reality in the forefront of his mind: "Martin Luther said that on his calendar were but two days: 'Today and That Day.' He recognized that all the days of his earthly existence were preparation for that momentous day when he would stand before a Holy God in eternity and give an account for his life."[7]

Now, I want to make sure you understand this. It is your foundation, your relationship with Christ, that determines whether or not you have a place in Heaven. How you spent your time and how you built your life determines your reward in Heaven. The judgment seat of Christ is an event ONLY for those who are Christ-followers.

But, as a Christ-follower, what you do in this life determines the reward of your life in eternity. Russell Crowe, as Maximus, was right in *Gladiator* when he said, "What we do in this life echoes in eternity."[8]

When it comes to giving rewards, God does not delegate the job. Michael the archangel doesn't hand out the crowns. The apostle Paul doesn't pass out the rewards. God Himself does the honors. Awards aren't given a nation at a time or a generation at a time. There is no need to hurry. God Himself will look you in the eye and bless you with His words, "Well done, good and faithful servant."

This passage in 1 Corinthians 3 closes with a sobering statement. Paul says,

> If what has been built survives, the builder will receive a reward. If it is burned up, the builder will suffer loss but yet will be saved—even though only as one escaping through the flames. (vv. 14–15)

If our sins are not being judged, then what does it mean, "he will suffer loss"? For many, this is a moment of sobering reality. For some Christians, it will be on this day that they realize that, even though they knew Christ, they lived for all the wrong things.

What a tragic day of regret to stand before Jesus, the lover of your soul, and realize that you squandered the one and only life you had here on earth.

These verses indicate that for many believers, this judgment will be a time of loss. They are not judged for their sin, but it will be a time of regret for many, because they will realize they wasted the life that God had entrusted to them.

> **What a tragic day of regret to stand before Jesus, the lover of your soul, and realize that you squandered the one and only life you had here on earth.**

It is the kind of loss someone might feel when they stand next to the judge's platform and watch others receive their rewards and realize they also could have had such a reward.

Paul describes this person who suffers loss as someone who barely made it out of a fire. They personally were saved, but that was it.

It reminds me of a story I read a few years ago about Dr. Bud Thompson. He was a seventy-nine-year-old stroke patient who was partially paralyzed after a plane crashed into his house in Dallas, Texas. The house immediately caught fire. His fifty-one-year-old caregiver rushed back into the burning and smoke-filled house and pulled Dr. Thompson to safety. He was rescued, but all his earthly possessions were gone.

Before we move on, let me remind you that how you steward your life today determines your reward in Heaven. So, in the words of the apostle Paul, "build with care."

7

HOW WILL HUMAN HISTORY *REALLY* END?

PART 2

Then I saw "a new heaven and a new earth," for the first heaven and the first earth had passed away, and there was no longer any sea. I saw the Holy City, the new Jerusalem, coming down out of heaven from God, prepared as a bride beautifully dressed for her husband. And I heard a loud voice from the throne saying, "Look! God's dwelling place is now among the people, and he will dwell with them. They will be his people, and God himself will be with them and be their God."

Revelation 21:1–3

As we begin chapter 7, let me encourage you to take a moment and look at the chart of events that God has made known to us as He brings His plans and purpose to fruition in this world. It's easy to get lost in the details and specifics of God's plan. I've found it very helpful to continually review the "Big Picture" as I study the unfolding of human history revealed in the book of Revelation.

PAST	PRESENT	FUTURE
Genesis 1–2	Genesis 3–Revelation 20	Revelation 21–22
Original mankind	Fallen mankind/Some believe and are transformed	Resurrected mankind
Original Earth	Fallen Earth with glimmers of original	New Earth; resurrected on mankind's coattails
God delegates Earth's reign to innocent mankind	Disputed reign with God, Satan and fallen mankind	God delegates Earth's reign to righteous mankind
Creation and mankind perfect	Creation and mankind tainted by sin	Creation and mankind restored to perfection
Mankind in ideal place	Mankind banished, struggles and wanders in fallen places	Man restored to ideal place, but much improved
God's plan for mankind and Earth revealed	God's plan for mankind and Earth delayed and enriched	God's plan for mankind and Earth realized

* Taken from Randy Alcorn, *Heaven* (Wheaton: Tyndale, 2004).

The other event that will happen sometime after the rapture is called the marriage supper of the Lamb. This will be a great party in Heaven celebrating the long-awaited union of Christ and His bride, the church.

This magnificent event is described in Revelation 19:1–2 and Revelation 19:6–9.

After this I heard what sounded like the roar of a great multitude
in Heaven shouting:

> "Hallelujah!
> Salvation and glory and power belong to our God,
>   for true and just are his judgments. . . ."

Then I heard what sounded like a great multitude, like the roar
of rushing waters and like loud peals of thunder, shouting:

> "Hallelujah!
>   For our Lord God Almighty reigns.
> Let us rejoice and be glad
>   and give him glory!
> For the wedding of the Lamb has come,
>   and his bride has made herself ready.
> Fine linen, bright and clean,
>   was given her to wear."

(Fine linen stands for the righteous acts of God's holy people.)

Then the angel said to me, "Write this: Blessed are those who
are invited to the wedding supper of the Lamb!" And he added,
"These are the true words of God."

We have all been to weddings. And at the best weddings, there is
a meal and reception after the ceremony. It's a party to celebrate
the coming together of a bride and a groom.

Well, that's exactly what happens here in Revelation 19. The
groom Jesus is now once and for all united with His bride, the
church. This is the mother of all wedding receptions. Think of

the most over-the-top wedding reception you have ever been to. The setting was spectacular, the music was excellent, the decorations were beautiful, and the food was exquisite. The marriage supper of the Lamb will be all of that and so much more. I love the fact that in Heaven we will eat good food, enjoy a fun celebration, and experience fellowship with friends.

While this magnificent banquet is happening in Heaven, the tribulation is playing out on earth. At the end of the seven years of tribulation, Christ physically returns to the earth. We usually refer to this event as the second coming of Christ. In the rapture, Christ comes in the clouds and snatches believers off the earth. But at the second coming, Jesus literally comes back to earth.

This is a coming of power and judgment. This second coming will be drastically different than the first coming of Jesus. The first coming of Jesus was about compassion and grace. Jesus came as the Savior of the world. The second coming of Jesus will be about justice and judgment. Jesus returns this final time not as Savior, but as the righteous Judge. The first coming was that of a helpless infant. The second coming will be that of a triumphant King.

> **Over and over throughout history, God has wooed and pursued people. He has offered forgiveness and salvation. But people have stiff-armed and rejected the gracious offer of God.**

Over and over throughout history, God has wooed and pursued people. He has offered forgiveness and salvation. But people have stiff-armed and rejected the gracious offer of God. And there is coming a day when He will return in righteous judgment.

Second Peter 3:3–9 talks about God's loving patience prior to that day:

> Above all, you must understand that in the last days scoffers will come, scoffing and following their own evil desires. They will say, "Where is this 'coming' he promised? Ever since our ancestors died, everything goes on as it has since the beginning of creation." But they deliberately forget that long ago by God's word the heavens came into being and the earth was formed out of water and by water. By these waters also the world of that time was deluged and destroyed. By the same word the present heavens and earth are reserved for fire, being kept for the day of judgment and destruction of the ungodly.
>
> But do not forget this one thing, dear friends: With the Lord a day is like a thousand years, and a thousand years are like a day. The Lord is not slow in keeping his promise, as some understand slowness. Instead he is patient with you, not wanting anyone to perish, but everyone to come to repentance.

Peter says that some scoff at the idea of Jesus coming again. Their rationale is that history just keeps marching on and nothing ever really changes. They mistake God's delay as a sign that He's not coming. But Peter tells us that the delay of Christ's return is a sign of patience and love. He says that God's heart is that He doesn't want anyone to perish and experience eternal judgment. But His patience is not limitless. That's why Peter says in verse 7 that there is a "day of judgment" coming. God's holy and righteous character demands justice, and eventually there will be a day of reckoning.

And deep down, because we are created in the image of God, we want a world that is just and a God who is just. Evil and sin must be judged. Everything in us recoils when we see injustice. When we see someone evil get off on a technicality, we are incensed. When we hear about ethnic cleansing or sex trafficking or terrorist attacks, we are outraged. Built into our DNA is the expectation of justice, because we are made in the image of God.

I was with a friend recently who shared with me about the mission work of one of his friends who sees evil and injustice up close and personal. This missionary works in Africa in a place that sits on the edge of a lake. Rebels will come by boat in the middle of the night and steal kids from their villages. They then take these children back across the lake where they cross the border and sell them into slavery. Well, this missionary is part of a very high-risk group that goes over the border and rescues these kids from a life of slavery and abuse. There is evil in the world, and all of our education, enlightenment, and technological advancement hasn't stopped it. Nor will it.

> **Built into our DNA is the expectation of justice, because we are made in the image of God.**

So to briefly recap, the *rapture* takes place when Christ comes and snatches believers off of the earth. That event is followed by seven years of tribulation on the earth. While the *tribulation* is happening on the earth the *judgment seat of Christ* and the *marriage supper of the Lamb* are taking place in Heaven. Following the completion of the tribulation, Jesus will come again back to the earth as king and ruler (this is referred to as *the second coming*). What happens next is the fulfillment of Jesus' promises to both Abraham and David.

1. Christ will rule and reign on the earth for 1,000 years.

After the seven years of tribulation and Jesus returns to the earth as judge, He will now be king over the earth. And He will establish His reign on earth for 1,000 years.

This period of time, called the millennium (which means 1,000 years), is described in Revelation 20:4–6:

> I saw thrones on which were seated those who had been given authority to judge. And I saw the souls of those who had been beheaded because of their testimony about Jesus and because of the word of God. They had not worshiped the beast or its image and had not received its mark on their foreheads or their hands. They came to life and reigned with Christ a thousand years. (The rest of the dead did not come to life until the thousand years were ended.) This is the first resurrection. Blessed and holy are those who share in the first resurrection. The second death has no power over them, but they will be priests of God and of Christ and will reign with him for a thousand years.

During this thousand years, Christ will replace the Antichrist as the ruler over the earth. Now, on the earth during the millennium there will be a very unique collection of people. First, there will be people who survive the tribulation and will enter the millennium in their earthly, physical, unglorified bodies. Second, there will be Old Testament saints and New Testament saints who now have their glorified bodies.

Some of the promises that God made thousands of years earlier will be fulfilled and realized during the millennium. Throughout the Bible, God has made many promises. And unlike us, He cannot break His promises. God's holy character prohibits Him from saying one thing and doing another. God made an outrageous promise to David that a descendant of his would sit on the throne forever. He made an outrageous promise to Abraham about a piece of land now called Israel and about a people called the Jews. Let me tell you, God has not forgotten His promises. Those unconditional promises made to Abraham and David will now be fulfilled.

As I have studied prophecy and the book of Revelation over the years, I've often wondered about this thousand-year reign upon the earth. To say it's unusual is an understatement, so much so that many will see this as merely a "period of time" and not a literal thousand years. Others will actually teach that this period has already happened or it is a "spiritual millennium" but not one that will actually happen on the earth.

I certainly respect the scholarship and views of others, but it seems that two great truths emerge from consistently interpreting this section of Scripture in the same way we do the rest of the Bible.

First, it provides a literal fulfillment of very specific and literal promises God made to David and Abraham. Second, it is a powerful polemic against the humanistic notion that mankind is basically good.

By contrast, something emerges during the millennium related to the nature of man that is quite mind-blowing. You see, when I was growing up, my parents were schoolteachers, so education was extremely important in my family. After dinner every night at my house, we scooted our plates to the middle of the table, and then we would sit and discuss great books and history and current events. The mindset taught and presumed in academia was that if we could just educate everyone and give them the proper training, we could rid the earth of many of its problems. If people could learn the right things and think correctly and become enlightened, then everything would be better. All of that thinking was based on the fundamental assumption that man is basically good and that man's challenges were the result of ignorance and lack of education. In spite of all the evil in the world, there is still a strong fundamental belief that mankind is basically good and that through education and technology, we will win the battle over evil and ignorance.

But what happens during the thousand-year reign of Christ will reveal the fallacy of such thinking. During the millennium, Jesus will literally and physically rule the earth. He will be here in the flesh, in all of His righteousness and holiness and majesty. It will be a perfect environment. Remember that some people will enter the millennium after surviving the tribulation. They will still be in their earthly bodies, so they will continue to have children. And their children will have children. Because it is a thousand years in length, there will be several generations of people born. And each of the people born with earthly bodies during the millennium will have a sin nature just like you and I do now. The Bible tells us that during this thousand-year reign of Christ on earth, Satan will be locked up in the abyss by Christ. So he will not be able to tempt mankind, or cause trouble and deceive people. At the end of the thousand years, Satan will be released for one final time before he is forever cast into the lake of fire.

After he is released, he will be free to tempt mankind much like in the Garden of Eden. He will persuade a significant portion of the population to choose to reject Christ and follow Satan. Now let that soak in for just a moment. . . . People who have lived in a totally righteous environment, with the best education, with perfect justice, and in the presence of Jesus Himself will still choose to turn away from the God who loves them and will reject Christ. That truly reveals the dark and sinful heart of man.

In spite of all the evil in the world, there is still a strong fundamental belief that mankind is basically good and that through education and technology, we will win the battle over evil and ignorance.

We all have a tendency to think we are better than we are. For all of our advancements and discoveries and inventions, we have never been able to eradicate the sinful nature of man. In fact, every time we invent something that is good and wonderful, someone finds a way to corrupt and pervert it and use it for evil. Think of the wonder of nuclear power and the destruction of nuclear weapons. Consider the genius of communication and knowledge on the web and the perversions and damage done when porn and deception flood the email inboxes of the world.

2. God will judge Satan, angels, and the wicked dead at the Great White Throne.

In Revelation 20:11–15 John writes,

> Then I saw a great white throne and him who was seated on it. The earth and the heavens fled from his presence, and there was no place for them. And I saw the dead, great and small, standing before the throne, and books were opened. Another book was opened, which is the book of life. The dead were judged according to what they had done as recorded in the books. The sea gave up the dead that were in it, and death and Hades gave up the dead that were in them, and each person was judged according to what they had done. Then death and Hades were thrown into the lake of fire. The lake of fire is the second death. Anyone whose name was not found written in the book of life was thrown into the lake of fire.

These are words that can make us uncomfortable. We don't talk much anymore about hell and eternal judgment. But the Bible does talk candidly about the reality of hell and eternal condemnation.

In his book *The Problem of Pain*, C. S. Lewis had such a great perspective on this issue: "I willingly believe that the damned are, in one sense, successful, rebels to the end; that the doors of hell are locked on the inside."[9]

God is loving and gracious and has provided an opportunity for forgiveness and salvation. People who end up in hell are there because they have rejected the provision of Christ on the cross.

God will and does respect our freedom of choice. He will not save us against our will. And if we make the decision to reject Christ, God will let us have our way.

If this area is a struggle for you, as it is for many, I encourage you to listen to or watch "Why I Believe in Life after Death," where I provide a more in-depth analysis on Heaven and hell. (Visit livingontheedge.org/afterdeath.)

> **God will not save us against our will. And if we make the decision to reject Christ, God will let us have our way.**

Evil is real. Despite our desires for all to end well for everyone, God is just, and justice must be required of ISIS, Stalin, and Hitler, as well as child abusers, sex traffickers, and a myriad of evildoers. His desire for them and for all of us is that we would turn from the evil inclinations of our hearts and receive new life and forgiveness through Jesus Christ; but the choice is ours.

By contrast, God's plan for those who admit their need, humble themselves, and turn in faith to Jesus is beyond spectacular.

3. The New Heaven will come down on the New Earth.

In his vision from God, John describes the New Heaven and New Earth in Revelation 21:1–3:

> Then I saw "a new heaven and a new earth," for the first heaven and the first earth had passed away, and there was no longer any sea. I saw the Holy City, the new Jerusalem, coming down out of heaven from God, prepared as a bride beautifully dressed for her husband. And I heard a loud voice from the throne saying, "Look! God's dwelling place is now among the people, and he will dwell with them. They will be his people, and God himself will be with them and be their God."

Revelation 21 introduces a new chapter when it comes to Heaven. Up until Revelation 21, Christians who have died have experienced Heaven, but it is different than the New Heaven talked about in Revelation 21. As I talked about earlier, theologians throughout the years have referred to Heaven prior to Revelation 21 as the Intermediate Heaven.

Once human history as we know it has been completed, this New Heaven will descend upon a New Earth. The New Heaven is both a country and a city.

We are going to spend the next couple of chapters taking a tour of the New Heaven and the New Earth. Get ready to be blown away by what God has prepared for you.

8

WHAT WILL OUR HOME IN HEAVEN *REALLY* BE LIKE?

And he carried me away in the Spirit to a mountain great and high, and showed me the Holy City, Jerusalem, coming down out of heaven from God. It shone with the glory of God, and its brilliance was like that of a very precious jewel, like a jasper, clear as crystal.

Revelation 21:10–11

In that great classic *The Wizard of Oz*, there is that memorable scene where Dorothy closes her eyes, clicks her heels, and utters those famous words, "There's no place like home . . . there's no place like home . . . there's no place like home."

I don't know what your memories of home are, but in the best families, the idea of home evokes deep and satisfying emotions. Home is where you belong. Home is where you are loved. Home is where you can be yourself. Home is comfortable. And your home reflects you. When home is right and good, there is something warm and secure about it.

For believers, Heaven is our ultimate home. And as the old hymn writer reminds us, this world is not our home . . . we're only passing through.

God has literally been preparing our home for us. It is called Heaven and it will be a place beyond our wildest imaginations. But let's be honest, it's a home we have never seen, and there are a lot of unknowns about our future home. If someone gives you a gift you've never seen, how do you really know if the gift will be as good as they tell you it is? There is only one way to know . . . and that is based on the trustworthiness of the person giving the gift. What is their track record? Do they have a history of telling the truth and delivering on their promises?

> **Home is where you belong. Home is where you are loved. Home is where you can be yourself.**

Though we have never seen or experienced Heaven yet, we can have full confidence about this great gift because of the trustworthiness of the One giving it to us. God has a long track record of telling the truth and delivering exceedingly and abundantly beyond what we could ever ask or imagine.

But still our curious minds want to know things like . . .

1. Will Heaven be an actual place?

2. What will we look like in Heaven?

3. Will Heaven be boring?

4. What will we do for all eternity?

5. Will animals be in Heaven?

6. Will my pet be there?

7. Will I have a mansion, an apartment, an efficiency condo?

8. Who gets to go to Heaven?

Theologians throughout the centuries have written much on these questions. For example, St. Thomas Aquinas thought we would all be thirty-three years old in Heaven. Others have made logical deductions and inferences that explain why animals will be there, and perhaps even your favorite pet. But there are certain things we just won't know until we get there. What I am trying to focus on in this book is, what does the Bible actually say about Heaven? There are lots of things we could speculate about and have opinions about. But they would be just that—speculations and opinions. The only authoritative source about Heaven is the Bible.

So, let's roll up our sleeves and answer the question, what will Heaven be like on the New Earth? That is not a typo or misprint.

The question is not, what will life be like on the New Earth? It is, what will Heaven be like on the New Earth?

When you come to the end of the Bible, in Revelation 21 and 22, earth and Heaven will merge. Faith will become sight. So, what will this New Heaven be like?

1. It will be a lot like the new me.

Remember that when Jesus comes in the rapture to "snatch away" believers off the earth, we will at that time be given our resurrected body. My new body will be glorified and perfect and suited for eternity. But the important thing to remember is that it is still me. My identity and the fundamental characteristics that make me Chip will still be in place. I will just be a new and very much improved Chip.

My new body will be like Christ's resurrected body. In 1 John 3:2, John writes, *"Dear friends, now we are children of God, and what we will be has not yet been made known. But we know that when Christ appears, we shall be like him, for we shall see him as he is."*

This is such an amazing promise. We don't know all the details of what it will be like to have a glorified body, but it is enough to know that we will be like Jesus.

When the apostle Paul talks about our glorified bodies in 1 Corinthians 15:44–49, he says,

If there is a natural body, there is also a spiritual body. So it is written: "The first man Adam became a living being"; the last Adam, a life-giving spirit. The spiritual did not come first, but the natural, and after that the spiritual. The first man was of the dust of the earth; the second man is of heaven. As was the earthly man, so are those who are of the earth; and as is the heavenly man, so also are those who are of heaven. And just as we have borne the image of the earthly man, so shall we bear the image of the heavenly man.

Paul makes one singular point. Adam had an earthly, physical body . . . but Jesus, the last Adam, had a glorified body. The bodies we have now are natural and of this earth. But our glorified bodies will be spiritual and of Heaven. When our bodies are resurrected, we will have a body like Jesus, the second Adam.

When our bodies are resurrected, we will have a body like Jesus, the second Adam.

There are a few things we know about Jesus' resurrected body. We know He definitely had some new capabilities. In Luke 24, after the resurrection, the disciples are having a meeting discussing their belief that Jesus had indeed risen from the dead. And in the middle of their discussion, Jesus just appears.

> While they were still talking about this, Jesus himself stood among them and said to them, "Peace be with you."
>
> They were startled and frightened, thinking they saw a ghost. (vv. 36–37)

117

It appears that Jesus no longer had the same limitations we have in our human, earthly bodies. It seems as though He can just appear and move from place to place without having to walk there. Jesus actually walked through walls and just appeared to the disciples that day. That's why it says in verse 37 that they were startled and frightened and thought they had seen a ghost. It was definitely Jesus, but He obviously had new capabilities with His resurrected body. Way before *Star Trek* and way before Captain Kirk ever uttered the words, "Beam me up, Scotty," Jesus was actually walking through walls and transporting Himself from one place to the next.

But we can also see from this same passage in Luke that Jesus still had an actual body that functioned much like our earthly bodies.

He said to them, "Why are you troubled, and why do doubts rise in your minds? Look at my hands and my feet. It is I myself! Touch me and see; a ghost does not have flesh and bones, as you see I have." (vv. 38–39)

His glorified body has hands and feet. Jesus even encourages them to touch Him and lets them know that a ghost wouldn't have flesh and bones. So it appears that Jesus' resurrected body looks very much and functions very much like our bodies now. Jesus also affirms that it is actually Him when He makes the statement, "It is I myself." And in your glorified body, you will still be you, but with some new and improved capabilities.

As one final proof that He is not just some ghost, He asks for something to eat.

When he had said this, he showed them his hands and feet. And while they still did not believe it because of joy and amazement, he asked them, "Do you have anything here to eat?" They gave him a piece of broiled fish, and he took it and ate it in their presence. (vv. 41–43)

He took it and ate it in their presence. I don't know about you, but I am glad we will be able to eat in our glorified bodies, and I am confident we won't have to worry about calories.

In the same way, the New Heaven and the New Earth will be a lot like our new and glorified bodies. There will be much that is familiar and similar to what we know in this life, but it will be infinitely better. Just as my body will be resurrected and made new, so the earth will be restored. You will have a new body suited for the New Heaven. Everything you have experienced in this life and everything you love about this earth is just a glimpse of what is to come.

Think about the most spectacular sunset you have ever witnessed. Think about your favorite place to vacation. Think about the greatest adventure you've ever been on. Think about your favorite memory with your kids. The New Heaven and the New Earth will be all of that and so much more.

What the Bible teaches is, *as man was, so was the earth. As man fell, so did the earth. As man will be, so will be the New Earth.*

In other words, when God originally created Adam and Eve, they were perfect. They were perfectly suited for the perfect environment of the Garden of Eden. When man fell and sin entered the world, the earth also fell. And just as we have been marred and scarred by sin, so has the earth. But there is coming a day when we will receive glorified bodies and we will be delivered from sin. And the same is true of the earth. There is coming a day when the earth will be restored and made new, and the New Heaven will come down on the New Earth.

> **As man was, so was the earth. As man fell, so did the earth. As man will be, so will be the New Earth.**

Seven hundred years before Christ, Isaiah would prophesy about this New Heaven and New Earth: "See, I will create new heavens and a new earth. The former things will not be remembered, nor will they come to mind" (Isa. 65:17).

God promises that there is going to come a day when He puts us back in a perfect environment just like the original environment.

The *Zondervan Pictorial Encyclopedia of the Bible* has a very interesting article on the New Heaven and New Earth:

> The New Heaven and the New Earth is a way of referring to the new creation that will come about at the end of time. The theme of the restoration and re-creation of the world is a central aspect of Christian hope. The returning of something, restoration to its original state, the redeeming work of Jesus Christ, both of humanity and all of creation, eventually that it will be restored is at the heart of God's plan.[10]

2. It will be a lot like the first earth.

The New Heaven and the New Earth will be familiar to us. In Genesis, God created the Garden of Eden and placed it on the earth. When Adam and Eve sinned, they were expelled from the garden, but they were still here on this earth. When Jesus left Heaven and was born in Bethlehem, He came to this earth. When you get to Revelation 21, there is a New Heaven and New Earth. It is still this same earth, but it has been restored and the curse of sin is removed.

At Wimbledon, the most important tennis matches are played at center court. It is the big stage. In history, planet Earth is center court. There are many other planets and galaxies, but God chose Earth to be center court. It is the big stage where His redemptive story would be played out. Because of sin, center court (Earth) has now been corrupted. But someday that will change. The Bible says that the old earth will pass away but is not annihilated. God is going to cleanse it and purify it and make it new.

Just think of your salvation. In 2 Corinthians 5:17 Paul says, *"Therefore, if anyone is in Christ, the new creation has come: The old has gone, the new is here!"*

Like the old me passed away, so the old earth will pass away. The old Chip passed away when I came to Christ. But there is a lot about the new Chip that looks strikingly similar to the old Chip. When I became a Christian, I still looked the same. My basic personality stayed the same. And I was still Chip Ingram.

Similarly, the New Earth will be new, better, different, but with continuity from the old earth.

Think for a few moments about what was true of the Garden of Eden. It was a perfect environment, with a tree of life. The same will be true of the New Heaven and the New Earth. It will be absolutely perfect, and according to Revelation 22:1–2, there will be a great river running through the New Heaven, and on each side of the river there will be a tree of life.

Just like the Garden of Eden, there will be water and trees and fruit and food. Animals will be there, but they will live in absolute harmony. There will be incredible natural beauty for us to enjoy. In the Garden of Eden there was no death and no shame, and the curse of sin was absent. There was no sorrow and no pain. Adam and Eve were given meaningful work to accomplish. They had purpose in their lives. And best of all, there was absolute intimacy with God and with each other. Dysfunction and isolation and shame weren't in the dictionary yet.

PAST	PRESENT	FUTURE
Genesis 1–2	Genesis 3–Revelation 20	Revelation 21–22
Original mankind	Fallen mankind/Some believe and are transformed	Resurrected mankind
Original Earth	Fallen Earth with glimmers of original	New Earth; resurrected on mankind's coattails
God delegates Earth's reign to innocent mankind	Disputed reign with God, Satan and fallen mankind	God delegates Earth's reign to righteous mankind
Creation and mankind perfect	Creation and mankind tainted by sin	Creation and mankind restored to perfection
Mankind in ideal place	Mankind banished, struggles and wanders in fallen places	Man restored to ideal place, but much improved
God's plan for mankind and Earth revealed	God's plan for mankind and Earth delayed and enriched	God's plan for mankind and Earth realized

Taken from Randy Alcorn, *Heaven* (Wheaton: Tyndale, 2004), 82.

That is a picture of the Garden of Eden, and the New Heaven and the New Earth will be very much like that. Are you starting to realize what hope and comfort and encouragement you've missed by the church's failure to teach about Heaven and by Hollywood's misrepresentation of our final home? Heaven is a real place with exquisite beauty and meaningful work and intimate relationships and good food and no death. There is nothing in Revelation 21 and 22 about floating on clouds and long white robes and harps.

No! The New Heaven and the New Earth will feel familiar, recognizable, and exceedingly awesome to us.

9

WHAT WILL MY LIFE IN
HEAVEN *REALLY* BE LIKE?

"'He will wipe every tear from their eyes. There will be no more death' or mourning or crying or pain, for the old order of things has passed away." He who was seated on the throne said, "I am making everything new!" Then he said, "Write this down, for these words are trustworthy and true."

Revelation 21:4–5

For centuries mankind has been fascinated and intrigued by Heaven. Poets have written about it, musicians have written songs about it, and artists have painted their ideas about it.

In our modern culture, there is a lot of speculation and conjecture about the afterlife. Books, movies, and activities about

Heaven seem to be everywhere. But what do *you* think Heaven is like? And what do you base your perspective on? And more importantly, what source are you going to trust?

I am not trying to invalidate anybody's personal experience. But I don't think I want to bank my understanding of Heaven on somebody's personal testimony. There are so many different versions, how would you know which one to trust?

The one authoritative source for our understanding of Heaven is the Bible. Throughout this book we have been discovering what the Bible actually says about Heaven. In this chapter we are going to discover some aspects of the New Heaven and New Earth that will be quite different than our experience in this life. As we have talked about, the New Heaven and the New Earth will be a lot like the new me and it will be a lot like the earth we currently live on. So there is familiarity and similarity, but there are going to be some things that make Heaven radically different than our life on earth.

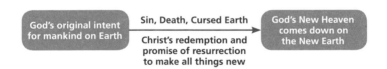

The New Heaven and New Earth will be very different and infinitely better because we will have . . .

A new relationship with God

Then I saw "a new heaven and a new earth," for the first heaven and the first earth had passed away, and there was no longer any sea. I saw the Holy City, the new Jerusalem, coming down out of heaven from God, prepared as a bride beautifully dressed for her husband. And I heard a loud voice from the throne saying, "Look! God's dwelling place is now among the people, and he will dwell with them. They will be his people, and God himself will be with them and be their God." (Rev. 21:1–3)

In the New Heaven and New Earth, God will be with us in a way that we have never experienced in this world. We will have a "face-to-face" relationship. In the New Heaven and New Earth, our faith will now be sight. I love how the passage says that God Himself will be with us. In this life, God has given us the indwelling of the Holy Spirit as a gift. The Holy Spirit comforts, convicts, guides, fills, teaches, and helps us as we seek to live the Christian life.

You know how you get that subtle prompting . . . and you struggle to try to figure out the will of God. At times I sense the Holy Spirit is prompting me, but it isn't always clear. The truth is that sometimes it is hard to discern the voice of the Spirit in our lives.

That will be a thing of the past. You will know the will of God 100 percent of the time, because you will be with Him.

In Heaven, you will never have any more days where it will be unclear or you wonder what God wants you to do. You will never have any cloud or doubt around God speaking to you.

You have probably experienced times in your journey where God has felt distant. Maybe there have been entire seasons where you felt like your prayers weren't getting above the ceiling. But in the New Heaven and New Earth, you will never feel distant or disconnected from God.

Certainly there have been times in your life when your fellowship with God has been broken. If you are truly born again, you are always a part of His family, but there are times and seasons when you experience a wall between you and God. Usually it is the result of sin and rebellion. In the New Heaven and New Earth, there won't ever be any barrier between you and God.

If you are like me, there have been plenty of times when you couldn't figure out what God was up to. Maybe there have been times when you were confused or even angry at God. His ways were unclear and maybe didn't make sense. In Heaven that will never be the case. You will understand the ways of God like never before.

> Maybe there have been entire seasons where you felt like your prayers weren't getting above the ceiling. But in the New Heaven and New Earth, you will never feel distant or disconnected from God.

God says, "I gave my Son for you. I love you, and you are the pinnacle of My creation. And I want an intimate, open, deep love relationship with you. The reason I created this Heaven is so that we could be together . . . forever."

There will be lots of new and different things in Heaven, but one that I'm most excited about is something that won't be there.

A new kind of relationship with sin

You will have a new relationship with your past. All the consequences of sin and evil are going to be removed, not just for you in your life, but for all of mankind.

> "'He will wipe every tear from their eyes. There will be no more death' or mourning or crying or pain, for the old order of things has passed away." He who was seated on the throne said, "I am making everything new!" Then he said, "Write this down, for these words are trustworthy and true." (Rev. 21:4–5)

Sin and brokenness are so ingrained in the fabric of our lives that I think it is hard for us to really conceive of a life and world without it. Can you imagine a world where there will be no abuse, no regrets, no betrayal, no divorce, no failure, no disappointment?

> **Can you imagine a world where there will be no abuse, no regrets, no betrayal, no divorce, no failure, no disappointment?**

You will never again experience the pain of rejection. There will be no more greed or murder or addictions. No more dishonesty. No more corruption. No more prejudice and racism. No more poverty. No more injustice. No one will ever be neglected again. No more fear. No more shame.

Just think about how much time and energy you spend in trying to resist temptation. Think about all of the emotional energy that goes into dealing with the consequences of your sin or dealing with sin in somebody else's life.

There won't be a need for policemen or lawyers. There won't be a need for a criminal court system or a prison system. Imagine a culture or society where sin didn't exist. That is the New Heaven and New Earth. But it doesn't stop there. This New Heaven doesn't just remove evil, it adds what we've all always longed for.

A new and complete satisfaction

> He said to me: "It is done. I am the Alpha and the Omega, the Beginning and the End. To the thirsty I will give water without cost from the spring of the water of life. Those who are victorious will inherit all this, and I will be their God and they will be my children. But the cowardly, the unbelieving, the vile, the murderers, the sexually immoral, those who practice magic arts, the idolaters and all liars—they will be consigned to the fiery lake of burning sulfur. This is the second death." (Rev. 21:6–8)

We all know the stress of dropping into bed at night after a long, hard day and having that feeling of still not being done. Maybe it's a big project we've been working on at work or repairing our car or finishing a term paper. In this life, it seems like we are never done. There is always more to do and our "to do" list never seems to go away. But in the New Heaven and the New Earth, God says, "It is done." There is such relief in knowing that someday it will all be done. It is complete. History has been written. God's purposes have been fulfilled and sin has been removed. God is now with us and the story of redemption is DONE.

God has made us to thirst, and He says that, to the thirsty, He will give water. He will quench our thirst. We certainly have physical thirsts, but He has given us other thirsts as well. We thirst for significance, security, love, acceptance, and fulfillment.

There is something inside of us that longs for significance. We want to feel like we matter. These are God-given thirsts. And the world we live in plays to those thirsts. The world markets to our thirsts. Secular companies have made billions of dollars marketing to our thirsts.

Our world system tells us that if we look a certain way or wear certain clothes or drive a certain car or vacation in a certain place or find the right person, then our thirsts will be quenched.

C. S. Lewis put it well: "When it comes to fame and celebrity and money and success and art and music and athletics, even when we achieve what we think is the ultimate . . . something is still missing."[11]

I think we have all experienced this when it comes to making a major purchase, especially something we've always wanted. For many, it's getting a new car. You save your money and you start shopping around. You visit dealerships and test-drive a few cars. You finally make a decision, sign the paperwork, and then comes that wonderful moment when they hand you the keys. It is yours! You are so excited and can't wait to show your friends. And for a few days or weeks you are completely jazzed about your new car.

But then, in a very short time, the shine has worn off. It is now just another thing you have to take care of and maintain. The satisfaction is very short-lived. For others, it could be going on an exotic vacation, or finally retiring, or buying a home. It's great you are happy for a season, but it doesn't deliver like you thought it would.

I love C. S. Lewis's profound perspective in his book *Mere Christianity*, when he writes,

> The Christian says, "Creatures are not born with desires unless satisfaction for those desires exists. A baby feels hunger: well, there is such a thing as food. A duckling wants to swim: well, there is such a thing as water. Men feel sexual desire: well, there is such a thing as sex. If I find in myself a desire which no experience in this world can satisfy, the most probable explanation is that I was made for another world. If none of my earthly pleasures satisfy it, that does not prove that the universe is a fraud. Probably earthly pleasures were never meant to satisfy it, but only to arouse it, to suggest the real thing. If that is so, I must take care, on the one hand, never to despise, or to be unthankful for, these earthly blessings, and on the other, never to mistake them for the something else of which they are only a kind of copy, or echo, or mirage. I must keep alive in myself the desire for my true country, which I shall not find till after death; I must never let it get snowed under or turned aside; I must make it the main object of life to press on to that country and to help others to do the same."[12]

I'm always struck by his statement, "Earthly pleasures were never meant to satisfy it, but only to arouse it, to suggest the real thing." Our thirsts will never be completely quenched in this life. And our pursuit of our thirsts has left a lot of us unsatisfied and frustrated and broken. As Lewis said, they are meant to simply arouse and suggest there is still something to come that will ultimately quench our thirsts.

Revelation 21 says that it is the coming of the New Heaven and the New Earth that will finally quench all of our thirsts. And for the first time we will be completely and utterly satisfied.

> You will never look over and want to be someone else. You will never compare yourself to someone else. You will never wish you were like someone else. You will be totally and completely satisfied.

You will never look over and want to be someone else. You will never compare yourself to someone else. You will never wish you were like someone else. You will be totally and completely satisfied.

In verse 7 of Revelation 21 God reiterates that He will be our God and we will be His children. It is easy to put all of the emphasis on the beauty and splendor and advantages of the New Heaven and New Earth, but I really believe that the signature quality of this perfect environment will be the intimate, open, connected, face-to-face relationship we will have with God. And like any good father, He wants His children to know and enjoy one another.

A new city and people to enjoy

In Revelation 21:1 John says that he sees the New Heaven and the New Earth. And then in verse 2, John sees *"the Holy City, the new Jerusalem, coming down out of heaven from God."* It is a massive and amazing city.

We also learn in Revelation 21 that there is no sea. For those of you who love to sail, I am sure there will be plenty of big lakes for you. But seas have always divided nations, and the sea has usually been seen as a fearful place. And you can't drink seawater. So, apparently in the New Heaven, there will only be freshwater.

Then, this amazing city called the New Jerusalem is unveiled. And it is unlike any other city in history.

> One of the seven angels who had the seven bowls full of the seven last plagues came and said to me, "Come, I will show you the bride, the wife of the Lamb." And he carried me away in the Spirit to a mountain great and high, and showed me the Holy City, Jerusalem, coming down out of heaven from God. It shone with the glory of God, and its brilliance was like that of a very precious jewel, like a jasper, clear as crystal. It had a great, high wall with twelve gates, and with twelve angels at the gates. On the gates were written the names of the twelve tribes of Israel. There were three gates on the east, three on the north, three on the south and three on the west. The wall of the city had twelve foundations, and on them were the names of the twelve apostles of the Lamb.
>
> The angel who talked with me had a measuring rod of gold to measure the city, its gates and its walls. The city was laid out like a square, as long as it was wide. He measured the city with the rod and found it to be 12,000 stadia in length, and as wide and high as it is long. The angel measured the wall using

human measurement, and it was 144 cubits thick. The wall was made of jasper, and the city of pure gold, as pure as glass. The foundations of the city walls were decorated with every kind of precious stone. The first foundation was jasper, the second sapphire, the third agate, the fourth emerald, the fifth onyx, the sixth ruby, the seventh chrysolite, the eighth beryl, the ninth topaz, the tenth turquoise, the eleventh jacinth, and the twelfth amethyst. The twelve gates were twelve pearls, each gate made of a single pearl. The great street of the city was of gold, as pure as transparent glass.

I did not see a temple in the city, because the Lord God Almighty and the Lamb are its temple. The city does not need the sun or the moon to shine on it, for the glory of God gives it light, and the Lamb is its lamp. (vv. 9–23)

God creates this new city for us to enjoy that is brilliant and beautiful. And all of God's people who have been redeemed will be there—Old Testament saints and New Testament saints.

John says that the New Jerusalem is 12,000 stadia in length, width, and height. Now, we are not used to thinking of things in terms of "stadia." Are you ready for this? Twelve thousand stadia is about 1,400 miles. So this city is 1,400 miles wide, 1,400 miles long, and 1,400 miles high.

Not counting the height of the city, the New Jerusalem is 1,960,000 square miles. Just to put that into perspective, Los Angeles is 503 square miles. Hong Kong is 426 square miles. New York City is 469 square miles. And São Paulo is 588 square miles.

There are some cities in the world that really are amazing. Cities can be glorious things. I love Chicago. If you have ever walked downtown on Michigan Avenue or seen the beautiful skyline, you know what I am talking about. There are great museums and fabulous restaurants. There is theater and culture and beauty.

Hong Kong is another favorite city of mine. It doesn't matter what time of day or night, it is bustling with life and activity. In Hong Kong you have a unique blend of the most modern and the most ancient. You have a mixture of British influence and Chinese influence. It is a wonderful place to visit.

> **The signature quality of this perfect environment will be the intimate, open, connected, face-to-face relationship we will have with God.**

Maybe you have a favorite city you like to go to. What mankind has been able to create in cities throughout the centuries is nothing short of spectacular. Who would have ever dreamed of indoor skiing in Dubai? But even that is nothing compared to this city that God has created called the New Jerusalem.

In this massive city there are three gates on each side and an angel guarding each gate. That's pretty impressive. And because of our resurrected bodies, we may not need an elevator, but could you imagine an elevator that goes all the way to the top of the city? You talk about a spectacular view. I did a little calculation and an elevator that would go all the way up to the top of the city would have about 740,000 floors.

And as impressive as the size of the city is, what about the people that we will get to meet and hang out with? We will have limitless time in a real city with real people from every era of history. And we will get to hear the great stories of the Bible from people who actually lived it. And they will be able to fill in the gaps and provide the color commentary that we just can't get by reading the Bible.

And then notice there is no sun or moon. Heaven's power comes directly from Jesus, and the glory of God is more than enough to light all of Heaven.

You will never be bored. There will be so much to enjoy and see and do and experience.

In verse 22 John says there is no temple in the New Jerusalem. Then, interestingly, he says that God the Father and Jesus are its temple. In the Bible people would go to the temple to encounter God and to meet with Him. In Heaven there will be no need for that because we will be with Him. We will be in constant union and communion with God. We will have a face-to-face relationship with the God and Creator of the universe.

The New Heaven and the New Earth are not limited to just the New Jerusalem. There will be other nations and kings.

A New Earth with new nations

The nations will walk by its light, and the kings of the earth will bring their splendor into it. On no day will its gates ever be shut, for there will be no night there. The glory and honor of the nations will be brought into it. Nothing impure will ever enter it, nor will anyone who does what is shameful or deceitful, but only those whose names are written in the Lamb's book of life.

Then the angel showed me the river of the water of life, as clear as crystal, flowing from the throne of God and of the Lamb down the middle of the great street of the city. On each side of the river stood the tree of life, bearing twelve crops of fruit, yielding its fruit every month. And the leaves of the tree are for the healing of the nations. No longer will there be any curse. The throne of God and of the Lamb will be in the city, and his servants will serve him. They will see his face, and his name will be on their foreheads. There will be no more night. They will not need the light of a lamp or the light of the sun, for the Lord God will give them light. And they will reign for ever and ever. (Rev. 21:24–22:5)

If you have nations, you have organization and infrastructure. If you have kings, you have roles and authority and jobs. If the glory of nations is brought to the city, that means there is commerce, art, culture, music, and manufacturing.

We can sometimes reduce worship down to singing songs and listening to a sermon for an hour on Sunday. But worship is so much more than that. Part of our worship is doing what we were made to do for the glory and the pleasure of the One who created and gifted us to do it.

Do you remember the movie *Chariots of Fire*? It is the story of Eric Liddell, a Scottish runner in the 1924 Olympics. In one of the great lines in the movie, Liddell says, "I believe God made me for a purpose, but He also made me fast. And when I run I feel His pleasure."[13]

In this New Heaven and New Earth, you will do what you are gifted to do and passionate about—but without sin and comparison and mixed motives.

And when you do that, you will do it in worship to God . . . which, by the way, is exactly what He wants from us today.

We are called to be living sacrifices. When you go to work and do a good job and tell the truth and love people, that is living a life of worship. When you humbly and unselfishly serve your family, that is living a life of worship. When you generously bless someone else and meet a need, that is living a life of worship. And we are going to do those same kinds of things in Heaven. We will serve and use our gifts and be useful to others and to God. You won't just be lying around on a hammock for all of eternity. You will live life to the fullest!

Our roles in Heaven will be determined according to Jesus by how we lived on this earth. God gave to each of us a certain amount of time and treasure and talent. And how we steward our lives here will determine our reward and our role in Heaven.

I hope you are beginning to get a little excited and enthusiastic about what is waiting for us on the other side of death. I hope that when you think of Heaven, your heart begins to beat just a little faster and you actually look forward to going there.

We have all seen the commercials about Disney World and Disneyland. Their tagline is that it is the happiest place on earth. But I've got news for you. When Heaven comes down on earth . . . that will be the happiest and greatest place on earth.

10

HOW CAN I *REALLY* LIVE TODAY IN LIGHT OF TOMORROW?

Therefore we do not lose heart. Though outwardly we are wasting away, yet inwardly we are being renewed day by day. For our light and momentary troubles are achieving for us an eternal glory that far outweighs them all. So we fix our eyes not on what is seen, but on what is unseen, since what is seen is temporary, but what is unseen is eternal.

2 Corinthians 4:16–18

So, why go to all this trouble to understand the Garden of Eden, the New Heaven, the New Earth, and the Intermediate Heaven? Is it just helpful information about my future home? Or does my understanding of Heaven actually impact how I live here and now? I'm sure you've heard the old adage, "he's so heavenly minded, he's no earthly good." Well, I'd suggest that just the opposite is true. Gaining a clear and compelling view of my "tomorrow" in Heaven changes how I live my "today" here on earth.

1. An accurate view of Heaven provides perspective in times of trouble and suffering.

In the following passage in 2 Corinthians, the apostle Paul has been imprisoned, persecuted, beaten, and left for dead. If we had been through such trials, we certainly would have been devastated and depressed. But not Paul. Listen to the hope and perspective he has as he walks through the worst that life and Satan can throw at him:

> Therefore we do not lose heart. Though outwardly we are wasting away, yet inwardly we are being renewed day by day. For our light and momentary troubles are achieving for us an eternal glory that far outweighs them all. So we fix our eyes not on what is seen, but on what is unseen, since what is seen is temporary, but what is unseen is eternal. (2 Cor. 4:16–18)

In verse 14, Paul declares his confidence that just as God raised Jesus from the dead, we will one day be raised as well. In other words, Paul is saying that this life is not all there is. Our eternity in Heaven is as certain as our life on this planet. That's why Paul begins verse 16 with the word "therefore." The word "therefore" always points us back. Because our resurrection and eternal future is secure, "therefore" we don't have to lose heart.

When you get a clear picture of your future, it will change your perspective of your trials and struggles today. It's like the analogy used by C. S. Lewis. All of eternity can be compared to a continuous line that has no beginning and no end, and all of human history is like a tiny dot on that line. And inside the dot of human history there is a microscopic dot that represents all of your life here on this earth. So, the question I want to ask you is, are you living for the dot or for the line?

I don't know about you, but I don't want to get to the end of my life and have a long list of regrets. I don't want to come to the end of my days and realize that I only lived for the dot, the temporal, the now, instead of for the line, the eternal, the forever.

When you get a clear perspective on Heaven, you think differently; you think wisely. This world doesn't have the same hold on you when you realize that your life transcends the dot. When your perspective gets clear, your priorities become clearer as well. You know what to say yes to and what

Are you living for the dot or for the line?

to say no to. So don't blow it. Let me encourage you—don't be cajoled, manipulated, hoodwinked, or seduced into living for the dot. With your one and only life, live for the line. You'll never regret it!

Notice that in verse 17 Paul refers to our troubles as "light and momentary." By anybody's standards we would not have described Paul's trials as light and momentary. In 2 Corinthians 11, Paul makes a list of his trials and suffering.

> I have worked much harder, been in prison more frequently, been flogged more severely, and been exposed to death again and again. Five times I received from the Jews the forty lashes minus one. Three times I was beaten with rods, once I was pelted with stones, three times I was shipwrecked, I spent a night and a day in the open sea, I have been constantly on the move. I have been in danger from rivers, in danger from bandits, in danger from my fellow Jews, in danger from Gentiles; in danger in the city, in danger in the country, in danger at sea; and in danger from false believers. I have labored and toiled and have often gone without sleep; I have known hunger and thirst and have often gone without food; I have been cold and naked. (vv. 23–27)

Yet, in spite of all that he had been through, he would still call them "light and momentary." How could Paul have such an amazing perspective? The answer is found in Romans 8: *"I consider that our present sufferings are not worth comparing with the glory that will be revealed in us"* (v. 18).

Compared to the glory that awaits us in Heaven, even Paul's long list of trials can be considered "light and momentary." You see, Paul was one of those rare people who got a glimpse of Heaven (2 Cor. 12:2–4), and that glorious experience gave him a new lens to compare everything else in life. Interestingly, he was prohibited from talking about what he saw.

The supreme example of this truth is Jesus Himself:

For the joy set before him he endured the cross, scorning its shame, and sat down at the right hand of the throne of God. Consider him who endured such opposition from sinners, so that you will not grow weary and lose heart. (Heb. 12:2–3)

I love those words "for the joy set before him." Jesus found the ability to look beyond the cross and see the joy that was coming. One of the advantages that Jesus has over us in our suffering is that He had been in Heaven. He had experienced Heaven and knew exactly what awaited Him on the other side of the cross.

That's why the writer of Hebrews challenges us to not grow weary and lose heart. Beyond the sufferings of this world is an unspeakable joy that will be ours to experience.

2. An accurate view of Heaven provides perseverance in times of temptation.

When the tough times come, and they will, if you don't have the right understanding of Heaven and eternity, you will be tempted to give up and give in. Jesus reassures His fear-filled disciples (and us) the night before His crucifixion with these words:

Do not let your hearts be troubled. You believe in God; believe also in me. My Father's house has many rooms; if that were not so, would I have told you that I am going there to prepare a place for you? (John 14:1–2)

143

I vividly remember the day a few years ago that we found out my wife had cancer. I could take you back to the spot where we sat on the couch and cried together. Praise God she is fine today, but I remember having this thought: "I'm not sure if I am going to have her with me much longer or not. And how am I going to deal with this?"

I remember stepping back and reminding myself that my experience and my theology tell me that God is good. She belongs to Him, and God has every right to take her to Heaven before me. And through my tears, I made a decision as to how I would respond. In that moment I decided that no matter what happened, from that point forward I would hold on to two fundamental truths . . . Heaven is real and God is good!

> **In that moment I decided that no matter what happened, from that point forward I would hold on to two fundamental truths . . . Heaven is real and God is good!**

Don't skip past Jesus' words, "You believe in God; believe also in me." Our ability to persevere is directly connected to our ability to trust in Jesus and believe that He has our future firmly in His hands. We all know intellectually that we are going to die, but something in the human psyche works overtime to deny that reality. But when we face the brutal fact of our mortality, we open our minds and hearts to begin thinking and processing life, pain, challenge, and temptation through the lens of eternity. This is exactly what Jesus was doing in John 14 on His last night with His disciples.

Jesus goes on to tell the disciples that His Father's house has many rooms and that He would never mislead them. Jesus had been there. He knew that Heaven was a real place and not some wishful thinking of a religious fairy tale. In that moment, He was telling His followers that their hope in Heaven was not a false hope, an idea, or a concept, but a real place with a real future.

My absolute conviction and clarity about eternity is what sustained me through that difficult season of finding out my wife had cancer.

You see, when you have a clear understanding about eternity and about Heaven, trials and trouble can shake you, but they can't break you. Because we hold to the fundamental conviction that this life is not all there is. We are not fatalistic nor do we believe that life is a series of random events. No! We believe there is a God and that He is good. We believe this life is not all there is, and we believe God is sovereignly orchestrating human history and our individual lives. And when that becomes not just a nice idea but also a conviction of your being, it changes everything.

> **When you have a clear understanding about eternity and about Heaven, trials and trouble can shake you, but they can't break you.**

3. An accurate view of Heaven provides clear priorities under pressure.

Jesus gave us some great insight about where to put our priorities in this life. In Matthew 6:19–20 He said,

> Do not store up for yourselves treasures on earth, where moths and vermin destroy, and where thieves break in and steal. But store up for yourselves treasures in heaven, where moths and vermin do not destroy, and where thieves do not break in and steal.

Storing up treasures for yourself on earth is a bad return on investment. Storing up treasures in Heaven is a wise investment. Did you notice that little phrase "for yourself"? Jesus' advice is investment counsel to benefit us when we reach our final and eternal home.

This passage tells us that what I do in this life actually impacts Heaven. It is like I have an account there, and as I live for eternal things and give my time and resources for eternal things, it is like I am wiring money ahead. Giving generously of your time and talent and treasure is an investment in your future in Heaven. And God is not a communist or a socialist. Heaven will be wonderful for everyone, but it will not be equal. What you do in this life will have direct impact on the quality of life in Heaven. No one will have a bad life in Heaven, but some will have greater reward than others. I encourage you to carefully read Jesus' teaching in the parable of the talents (Matt. 25). People were rewarded differently based on how they used what had been entrusted to them.

In 2 Peter, the apostle also talks about how our eternity should influence our priorities in this life. He says,

> But the day of the Lord will come like a thief. The heavens will disappear with a roar; the elements will be destroyed by fire, and the earth and everything done in it will be laid bare. Since everything will be destroyed in this way, what kind of people ought you to be? You ought to live holy and godly lives. (2 Pet. 3:10–11)

The world as we know it will not continue on forever. Jesus is going to return one day and everything will change. This old earth, ravaged by sin, will be replaced with a New Heaven and a New Earth. Peter adamantly declares that day is coming. It is a fact. It is certain. It is a day that God the Father has marked on His calendar. And in light of that reality, Peter says that we should live "holy and godly lives." Because God is the Sovereign Creator and His return is certain, it should motivate me to live a pure life and a life that reflects God's priorities. Temptation is real. The world's influence is powerful on all of us. Under pressure and in weak moments, we cave in and live with a selfish, temporal mindset—the results are predictable and painful. Jesus longs to give you His best and protect you from the consequences of misplaced

Heaven will be wonderful for everyone, but it will not be equal. What you do in this life will have direct impact on the quality of life in Heaven.

priorities. So let me ask you, what needs some attention in your life? Does your time, money, or activities reflect the holy and generous God you serve?

4. An accurate view of Heaven provides a proper view of possessions.

Jesus tells a very sobering story in the book of Luke. Even before He tells the story, He gives us the punch line. He is warning about greed, and He says, *"Life does not consist in an abundance of possessions"* (Luke 12:15).

Then He tells the story of a very successful and rich businessman who had an abundance of crops. That's a great problem to have. So, he needs a new plan. The world would call this guy a business guru. Yet God calls him a fool. For all his business savvy and entrepreneurial genius, he made a supreme miscalculation. In his frantic pursuit of the good life, he forgot to pursue eternal life and cultivate a rich relationship with God. He gave his life for that which ultimately didn't matter.

> In his frantic pursuit of the good life, he forgot to pursue eternal life. . . . He gave his life for that which ultimately didn't matter.

> Then he said, "This is what I'll do. I will tear down my barns and build bigger ones, and there I will store my surplus grain. And I'll say to myself, 'You have plenty of grain laid up for many years. Take life easy; eat, drink and be merry.'"

But God said to him, "You fool! This very night your life will be demanded from you. Then who will get what you have prepared for yourself?"

This is how it will be with whoever stores up things for themselves but is not rich toward God. (Luke 12:18–21)

This rich man began to live as though life and security were all about what you can accumulate in this life. God calls that kind of thinking foolish. The Bible is clear that an accurate view of eternity will cause me to hold possessions and material things loosely. That is so countercultural to our generation. We are obsessed with what we can acquire and possess. But when we begin to think about Heaven often, of what really matters and why, the stuff of this life will lose its grip on us.

> **An accurate view of eternity will cause me to hold possessions and material things loosely.**

There is a refrain to an old hymn that says it far better than I can:

> Turn your eyes upon Jesus,
> Look full in His wonderful face,
> And the things of earth will grow strangely dim,
> In the light of His glory and grace.[14]

That's a great truth and wise counsel, but how do you do it? How do we turn our eyes on Jesus and not get sucked into the black hole of materialism? Well, this isn't a new problem, and the apostle Paul, writing to his favorite son in the faith, instructs Timothy on how to win the battle with greed.

> Command those who are rich in this present world not to be arrogant nor to put their hope in wealth, which is so uncertain, but to put their hope in God, who richly provides us with everything for our enjoyment. Command them to do good, to be rich in good deeds, and to be generous and willing to share. In this way they will lay up treasure for themselves as a firm foundation for the coming age, so that they may take hold of the life that is truly life. (1 Tim. 6:17–19)

Notice the very specific commands in this passage.

Command those who are rich (in New Testament time, a rich person had more than one set of clothes and food for more than just today) *in this world . . .*

1. Not to be arrogant

2. Not to put their hope in wealth

Why? Because it is so uncertain, unreliable, and unable to deliver what matters most.

By contrast, they're commanded to . . .

1. Put their hope in God

2. Do good and be generous and willing to share

Why? Because He will richly supply us all with things (material and spiritual) to richly enjoy; and in doing so, we lay up for ourselves the treasure of a firm foundation of the kind of life, hope, and joy that's "really life."

In fact, by doing good, by sharing, and by being generous, I demonstrate that eternity is a priority. Generosity recalibrates my heart and allows me to store up treasure in Heaven rather than just building bigger barns for my stuff here on earth.

Please don't skip past the issue. We are all materialistic to some degree and it corrodes our soul. I want to challenge you to set aside a little time to consider the following questions: If I really believed and lived as though Heaven is real, what would need to change in my life? How would it impact your time? Your job? Your finances? Your relationships? Your thoughts?

11

ARE YOU *REALLY* TAKING HEAVEN SERIOUSLY?

Do not store up for yourselves treasures on earth, where moths
and vermin destroy, and where thieves break in and steal. But
store up for yourselves treasures in heaven, where moths and
vermin do not destroy, and where thieves do not break in and
steal. For where your treasure is, there your heart will be also.

Matthew 6:19–21

As we come to the end of our journey together, I'd like
to ask you three very important questions. We learned
that despite the mystery and unknown that surrounds
Heaven, there is much that we can know for certain; and it's
absolutely amazing.

A scriptural understanding of Heaven answers the biggest questions of life. Why am I here? What happens after I die? Why is there such evil in the world?

Heaven is a literal place, and the purpose of Heaven has been clear from the beginning. From the Garden of Eden, to the Intermediate Heaven, to the New Heaven on the New Earth, the purpose has always been the same—that God could be with us and we with Him in intimate communion.

Three Important Questions

God, the Creator of all life, wants to be with you forever. He made you, He loves you, and He sent Christ to pay for your sins and redeem you. You matter! You are valuable, precious, and extremely important to Him. He takes your life today and your future forever very seriously. So it only makes sense to close our time together by asking and answering three important questions to make sure we're taking Him and His Heaven seriously.

1. Are you certain that you are going to Heaven?

Our tendency is to get sucked into the daily grind of life—paying bills, returning emails, taking the kids to practice, getting the car repaired. And before you know it, your only thoughts are about this life and this world. We unconsciously forget that this world is not our home. If we could just grasp that Heaven is REAL and that by comparison, life here is nothing more than a dot on the line of eternity, it would change everything.

So, let me ask you a very personal question: Are you absolutely, 100 percent certain that if you died today, you would be ushered by angels into the presence of God?

The Bible is very clear that you can know the answer to this question for CERTAIN. It isn't about trying hard or being religious or hoping that it all works out. It isn't about giving to your favorite charity or attending church or doing good deeds. It is a gift of grace from a God who loves you and sent His Son to die in your place to pay for all your sins once and for all.

The apostle John writes,

> And this is the testimony: God has given us eternal life, and this life is in his Son. Whoever has the Son has life; whoever does not have the Son of God does not have life. I write these things to you who believe in the name of the Son of God **so that you may know** that you have eternal life. (1 John 5:11–13, emphasis added)

Listen to those words in verse 13. John says that he has written these things to those of us who believe so that we may *know* that we have eternal life. In fact, John writes in his gospel who actually qualifies for eternal life: *"Yet to all who did receive him, to those who believed in his name, he gave the right to become children of God"* (John 1:12).

The only question today about you and Heaven is, do you have the Son? It's not about you being a nice person or being sincere. It is about you making the conscious choice of your will to believe in Jesus and trust Him for your salvation.

Jesus said in John 14:6, *"I am the way and the truth and the life. No one comes to the Father except through me."* That is not my claim for Him; that is His claim for Himself. And either He was who He claimed to be or He is an impostor and a fraud.

But if you would believe (place your trust in Him) today, Jesus will forgive your sins and take up residence in your life today and guarantee you a spot in Heaven. You don't have to wait. You don't have to talk to a pastor. You don't have to go to a church to receive Christ. Right where you are, right now, you can choose to believe that Jesus is who He claimed to be. And you can choose to believe that He died on the cross for your sin, and right now you can ask Him to be your Lord and Savior. If you are

The Bible is very clear that you can know the answer to this question for CERTAIN.

not absolutely sure that you have eternal life, I invite you to take a few minutes to log on to livingontheedge.org/goodnews where I personally share God's love and plan for you. I've also included some much needed information and free resources to help you grow in your new life with Christ.

For many reading this book, the issue of your salvation has already been settled. You know with certainty that Christ is your Savior and He lives within by His Holy Spirit. But Heaven was never intended to be some vague idea that's simply nice to know about. A clear concept of Heaven, of eternal rewards, and of our certain future provides the basis and motivation to live a life that bears much fruit and prove to be His disciples (John 15:8). So with that in view, here is question number two:

2. Do your current priorities and passions reveal an eternal or temporal perspective?

One of Paul's favorite churches was the church at Philippi. Listen to his words as he challenges these early Christians to have an eternal perspective:

> Join together in following my example, brothers and sisters, and just as you have us as a model, keep your eyes on those who live as we do. For, as I have often told you before and now tell you again even with tears, many live as enemies of the cross of Christ. Their destiny is destruction, their god is their stomach, and their glory is in their shame. Their mind is set on earthly things.
>
> **But our citizenship is in heaven.** And we eagerly await a Savior from there, the Lord Jesus Christ, who, by the power that enables him to bring everything under his control, will transform our lowly bodies so that they will be like his glorious body. (Phil. 3:17–21, emphasis added)

One of the phrases he uses to describe those who don't live with an eternal perspective is "their god is their stomach." That is a phrase that is about appetites and passions for the stuff of this world. They live for the stuff they can acquire and consume now. They act and behave and make decisions as though this life is all there is. They are shortsighted in their perspective, and this accurately describes how so many people live in our generation. Their entire focus is on temporal pleasures and material possessions. They spend all of their energy and time trying to figure out how they can get "more." Unfortunately, this temptation was not reserved for first-century Christians. These are the kind of issues you and I face every day.

Paul goes on to say that they are people whose mind is set on earthly things. They are preoccupied with the temporal things of this world. They don't think about Heaven. The reality of eternity does not shape their decisions. Their treasure and what they really value is here on this earth. They are driven by the temporal rather than the eternal.

The truth is, it is very easy for us to get swept along in the flow of the culture. Everything around us puts the spotlight on temporal things like success, wealth, and looks. The gravitational pull of our culture is toward earthly things.

The word "but" in verse 20 is the pivot point for this passage. Paul is saying the world may live that way "but" we live differently. And we live differently because *our citizenship is in Heaven.* We are to have an eternal mindset. Our decisions and behaviors and thoughts should give testimony to the fact that we are "heavenly minded."

They don't think about Heaven. The reality of eternity does not shape their decisions. Their treasure and what they really value is here on this earth.

If we sat down together and reviewed each other's financials and looked over our calendars and could chart our thoughts over the last week, would there be any evidence that we are focused on eternal things?

Are you living today as though everything we have talked about in this book is true? If not, what would need to change? Please don't gloss over that last question. Sit quietly and honestly with those words for a few moments. Allow the Holy Spirit some space to speak to you. What would REALLY need to change for you to live with an eternal perspective?

> If we sat down together and reviewed each other's financials and looked over our calendars . . . , would there be any evidence that we are focused on eternal things?

My suspicion is that you won't get there with incremental change. You won't tweak things in your life and end up with a life focused on eternity. If your life is anything like mine, it might require you to make a radical shift. Whenever I've really stopped and contemplated Heaven and what really matters, it's always led to some midcourse changes. Months later, I realize that I've been pulled again back into the stream of "this world's" values and need to adjust again. I don't think this process will ever end. We are in a war and a battle for our souls and those we love. It doesn't mean we are bad people—it does mean we look through the lens of eternity and do whatever is necessary.

When I was a kid, there used to be a ride at the state fair that illustrates my point. You would walk into this big metal cylinder and stand against the wall. Then they would start spinning the cylinder, and when it got going fast enough, they would drop the floor out from under you. But the centrifugal force kept you pinned against the wall.

The same is true of our culture. The Bible calls it the "world's system" and it warns us that friendship with "the world," even as believers, makes us at odds with God (James 4:4–6). The centrifugal force of a culture focused on temporal things is so strong that if you don't do something radical, you will just keep spinning around like everybody else.

So, let me ask you, gently, one more time: What would have to change in your everyday life for you to live from a more eternal perspective? A life that reflected you really take Heaven seriously?

The final question I'd like you to ponder has to do with the eternal

> **Whenever I've really stopped and contemplated Heaven and what really matters, it's always led to some midcourse changes.**

destination of others. The Scripture is clear and absolute about the magnificent gift that awaits those who have received God's gracious and free offer through Christ. But the Bible is equally clear about the consequences of rejecting that offer.

It's very unpopular in our day to mention, let alone discuss, the reality of hell. Yet Jesus speaks about it often and with a view to it being as REAL and eternal as Heaven.

So with that in mind, let's tackle question number three.

3. Are there people you care about who don't know about Heaven or how to get there? How could God use you to help them?

When you think about the Heaven that Jesus has prepared for you as His child, are there people you know whom you care about deeply that are not on their way to Heaven? The truth is, they don't know Jesus personally and if they had a massive heart attack today, they would not go to Heaven.

Who do you think ought to tell them? Literally, their eternity is on the line. If everything we have talked about in this book is real and true, there is a lot at stake, not only in our lives, but also in the lives of the people we know and love. This issue is too important to be stifled by fear of what people will say or think. This matters too much for us to be silent because we are worried about being rejected. Even as I write these words, my logic and convictions say yes, but I still find myself being far less than bold on many occasions.

> **If everything we have talked about in this book is real and true, there is a lot at stake, not only in our lives, but also in the lives of the people we know and love.**

Why are we so fearful and so worried about being politically correct that we are paralyzed when it comes to sharing our faith? My concern for you and me is that we are going to have huge regret because we didn't share the good news with people that God put in our lives. Many of the people in our culture are not resistant to Jesus . . . they have just never lovingly and clearly heard the good news of the gospel. To be honest, I'm almost always shocked by how receptive people are and how God has already been working when I cast insecurities aside and share His love.

God has given you relationship and an open door with people that nobody else has. They trust you and you have credibility with them. You and I are God's plan for getting out the good news. He is not going to write it in the sky. He is not going to send angels to preach a sermon. God's only plan is for everyday believers like you and me to courageously look people in the eye and tell them that eternity is REAL and there is a God who loves them and wants to be with them. And through the death of Jesus on the cross God has already made a way for them to be saved and have a place in HEAVEN when they die.

> **God's only plan is for everyday believers like you and me to courageously look people in the eye and tell them that eternity is REAL.**

Here is the good news. It's not all up to you. As I shared earlier, God is already at work in the lives of our friends. God has a long history of pursuing those who are far from him. Luke 19:10 says, *"For the Son of Man came to seek and to save the lost."* He is using circumstances, success, failures, pain, fears, and deep longings, along with people like you and me, to draw them to Himself.

I love the words of 2 Samuel 14:14: *"All of us must die eventually. Our lives are like water spilled out on the ground, which*

cannot be gathered up again. But God does not just sweep life
away; instead, he devises ways to bring us back when we have
been separated from him" (NLT).

God devises ways to bring us to Himself when we have been
separated. So when it comes to sharing the good news, God
gives us the privilege of partnering with Him in His pursuit of
our friends.

When it comes to family, neighbors, co-workers, people at the
gym or the coffee shop, do they know that Heaven is real and
eternal life can be theirs? If you don't tell them, who will?

If you don't know or aren't quite sure where to begin, let me
be of help. I taught a series called Share the Love on how to
winsomely build relationships with nonbelievers in a way that
God has designed and gifted you. I then walk you through a
simple way to "tell your story" in a non-offensive but powerful
manner. Finally, I teach you how to share "His story," the gospel,
when your friend or family member asks, "How can I have a
relationship with God like you do?" I want to make this as easy
and convenient for you as possible. There is much at stake, and
whether we like it or not . . . we are perhaps the only Christian
they know. So go to livingontheedge.org/sharelove and down-
load both the notes and audio teaching free of charge.

When we consider how real and how wonderful Heaven is, how
could we not share the love?

APPENDIX A

WHY I BELIEVE THE BIBLE

The entire message of this book on Heaven rests on one foundational element: that the Bible is the inspired and infallible Word of God. Everything written in this book is based on the belief that the Bible is credible, trustworthy, and accurate.

But is that a valid assumption? Is there actual proof to suggest that the Bible is the Word of God? If we were to put the Bible on trial, what evidence would substantiate the claim of the Bible as the supernatural Word of God?

These are fair and honest questions, and anyone examining the claims of Christianity must settle the issue of the Bible's credibility. I am not asking you to simply take my word for it. Do your own research and investigation. If you're a skeptic or you're just unsure what you think, I want to challenge you to get a New Testament in an easy-to-read translation. And just read it with an open mind and say, "God, if You're real, speak to me."

That's what I had to do, because I grew up in a family and even went to a church that didn't take the Bible seriously. We had a Bible sitting on our coffee table, but we never read it and it had no impact on our family.

I was eighteen when I opened the Bible for the first time and began to seriously explore its teaching. It wasn't long before I committed my life to following Christ.

A friend taught me how to read the Bible in the mornings to begin to learn from this amazing book. My friend helped me understand that I wasn't just reading the Bible to learn information, I was reading to build relationship with the Author of the book. I also learned that God would speak to me and guide me through the Bible.

However, when I was in grad school, I had some very smart people challenge me about the intellectual basis of my faith. I remember one day having a conversation with one of the PhDs in grad school. He challenged my belief in the Bible and said, "You don't really believe that, do you?" My sheepish response was, "Well, yeah, I do." And then he said, "Well, why?" And I didn't have a good answer.

That moment started me on a journey to discover whether or not the Bible could be trusted. I found myself asking questions like . . . Is it really God's Word or is it simply the words of men? Is it simply another book of religious wisdom or is it truly inspired by God? What makes it different than other religious books? Is it historically accurate?

Let me give you a brief summary of my journey and the conclusions I came to after examining the evidence.

1. The Bible is historically accurate.

The people, places, and events have been historically and archaeologically verified. The stories of the Bible are not myths or fairy tales. For years liberal scholars pointed at a group in the Bible called the Hittites as proof that the Bible was historically inaccurate. There was no historical record or proof that the Hittites had existed. However, as a result of a later archaeological dig, they discovered 1,200 years of Hittite civilization.

In just the Old Testament alone, there are over 25,000 references to people and places that correspond with archaeological finds.

A famous historian and archaeologist by the name of Sir William Ramsay set out to prove that Luke's writings were filled with historical errors. He emerged from his investigation by saying Luke's history is unsurpassed in its trustworthiness.

Dr. Nelson Glueck is one of the greatest modern authorities on Israeli archaeology. He concludes, "No archaeological discovery has ever controverted a Biblical reference. Scores of archaeological findings have been made which confirm in clear outline or in exact detail historical statements in the Bible."[15]

2. The Bible claims to be the Word of God.

The Bible claims to infallibly reveal the very words and the mind of God. The Bible authoritatively claims that it is the Word of God. Second Timothy 3:16 says, *"All Scripture is God-breathed and is useful for teaching, rebuking, correcting and training in righteousness."*

The Bible actually claims to be the authoritative, inspired, infallible words of God. Over three thousand times in the Bible, you read "thus says the Lord." This isn't a good book with some good stories, with some good morals, to help people live a good life. This is the very mind and Word of God. This is God's will in printed form.

3. The Bible's origin is supernatural.

The Bible's unity, structure, and subject matter are different than any other book. The Bible was written by forty different authors in three languages over fifteen hundred years. The Bible was written in Hebrew, it was written in Aramaic, and it was written in Greek.

Author and former Moody Bible Institute instructor Terry Hall wrote a little article that's worth reading on how we got the Old Testament.[16] He said it had to be the strangest publishing project of all time. No editor or publishing house was responsible to oversee 40 independent authors, representing 20 occupations, living in 10 countries. It was written during a 1,500-year span, working in 3 languages, with a cast of 2,930 characters in 1,551 places.

Together they produce 66 books containing 1,189 chapters, 31,000 verses, 774,746 words, and 3,000,567 letters. This massive volume covers every conceivable subject, expressed in every kind of literary form, from prose to poetry, romance, mystery, biography, science, and history. What was the final product? The Bible. Our evidence that the Bible is a supernatural book is the unity it displays despite such wide differences among cultures, forms, and expressions. The Scripture's content, alignment, prophetic fulfillment, and connection over such a span of time and authorships reveal an invisible hand guiding the process and the ultimate product.

4. The life and person of Jesus validates the Bible.

I have served on two or three juries, and it is always intriguing. One of the keys in any trial is expert witnesses. You have someone who has done all this research and they're an expert in a particular field. It might be an expert psychologist or an expert in ballistics or forensics.

Because they are an expert, their testimony carries more weight than others. In the Bible, we have an expert witness and His name is Jesus. Jesus was different than any other person who ever lived. He did miracles and raised people from the dead. He even raised Himself from the dead. And as an expert witness, He believed that the writings of the Old Testament were God-inspired and were indeed the words of God.

5. Fulfilled prophecy authenticates the Bible.

This was probably the turning point for me. I didn't grow up in a Christian home and so I had never read the Bible. And when the teachings and claims of the Bible were challenged, it would shake my faith in the Scripture. But when I learned that the Bible contains hundreds of specific prophecies that had been specifically fulfilled, that was a game changer for me.

Some of the prophecies in the Bible were fulfilled hundreds of years later. Fulfilled prophecy is one of the clearest evidences that the Bible is supernatural and different than any other book ever written.

One of the most amazing prophecies is in Ezekiel 26, and it's a prophecy about the city of Tyre. You can read that for yourself, but let me summarize.

The prophecy had five points. It was prophesied that God will destroy the city of Tyre. Ezekiel prophesied that so many nations would come against Tyre that the city would become like a bare rock. This prophecy seemed absolutely ridiculous, as Tyre was a major city in its day and a center of trade and commerce.

This would be like someone today saying Chicago is going to be completely destroyed. You will go to Chicago and every building will be flattened. It'll never be rebuilt. It will be wiped off the map. I don't know about what you would think, but maybe a bomb or something could do that? It could happen. But even if it happened, I think we'd rebuild Chicago, wouldn't we? This is how outlandish this is.

The prophecy about Tyre was fulfilled exactly as Ezekiel had prophesied. It was absolutely demolished and never rebuilt.

The most powerful examples of fulfilled prophecy are all the prophecies about the Messiah. There are more than 300 specific predictions of Jesus coming His first time. It was prophesied that He would be born of a virgin, a descendant of Abraham, tribe of Judah, house of David, born in Bethlehem, and it was even predicted that John the Baptist would be His forerunner.

It was prophesied that He'd be mocked, beaten, spat on, betrayed, abandoned by His disciples. It was also predicted that He would have a triumphal entry, that He'd be a prophet, that He'd be crucified, that lots would be cast for His garments, that He would cry out from the cross, that no bones would be broken, that His side would be pierced, that He'd be buried with the rich, that He'd be resurrected and exalted, that He would ascend into heaven, and that He would sit at the right hand of God. Many of these predictions were made 700 years prior to His coming and described in detail. The crucifixion, which would not be invented as a means of execution until hundreds of years later, was described in detail.

Those are just a few of them. Those are all specific things that were said about this Messiah that will come as a reigning king and a suffering servant. Dr. Peter Stoner, author of the seminal book *Science Speaks*, says that by using modern science or probability in reference to eight prophecies, we find that the chance that any man fulfilling eight prophecies is one in ten to the seventeenth (10^{17}) power. And that's not for 300 prophecies . . . that's just for 8.[17]

Then he gives us this picture. He says, that would be like taking silver dollars and taking the entire state of Texas and stacking silver dollars two feet high and then taking one silver dollar and marking it and mixing it all up somewhere in Texas and then blindfolding a man and saying, "Okay, you can walk anywhere in Texas and you need to reach down and pick up that one silver dollar."

He said that is the probability of one man fulfilling 8 specific prophecies. And Jesus didn't fulfill 8. He didn't fulfill 28. He didn't fulfill 128. He fulfilled over 300 prophecies.

That's absolutely amazing! That was probably the tipping point in my life when I began to do the research and realize just how supernatural the Bible really is. If God can tell you what's going to happen in advance, you can trust what He's going to say about the present and about the future.

6. The manuscript evidence is overwhelming.

When you look at the number of manuscripts we have of the Bible compared to other writings, it is absolutely staggering. Let me just give you some examples to compare. The earliest copy we have of Plato's writing is dated at about AD 900; the time span from when he wrote it, back between 427 and 347 BC, to that earliest copy is about 1,200 years, and the number of copies we have of Plato's works is seven.

How about Aristotle? The earliest copy we have is from AD 1100. So it was 1,400 years after he lived before we have a copy of his writing.

What about Homer and the writing of *The Iliad* and *The Odyssey*? They were written around 900 BC, and the earliest copy is dated 400 BC. So it's only five hundred years between the time he lived and the earliest copies.

No one doubts the authenticity of Plato, Homer, or Aristotle. But what about the New Testament? It was written between AD 40 and 100, and our earliest copies are dated AD 125. Just twenty-five years after the writing of the New Testament was complete. People were still living who could authenticate what was going on. And how many copies do we have? We have over 24,000 manuscripts. Actually, 24,643, to be exact.

What we have is the most historically reliable, accurate document on the face of the earth.[18]

This journey has not been merely intellectual for me. It is highly personal. God, through the Bible, has transformed my life. With everything that is in me, I believe the Bible to be the inspired and infallible Word of God. It is God's letter to us. In it He reveals Himself to us and tells us how to live. Its teachings inform how I spend my money, how I raise my kids, how I treat people, what I value, how I do my job, and where I invest my time. I am staking my life and eternity on the truthfulness of the Bible. I hope you will do the same.

APPENDIX B

FAQ

1. Do babies go to Heaven?

The very short answer is "yes."

But the question raises very significant theological issues that we do not want to treat lightly. The best book or teaching on this subject to my knowledge is by Dr. Robert Lightner in his brief sixty-four-page book entitled *Heaven for Those Who Can't Believe*. He writes the following in chapter 4 as he frames the issue clearly:

> A review of the ground covered thus far is in order. Every human being is born in sin. All have sinned and fallen short of the glory of God (Rom. 3:23). "There is none righteous, no, not one" (Rom. 3:10). All are "objects of wrath" at birth (Eph. 2:3,

NIV). The Lord Jesus Christ made provision for the salvation of all in His substitutionary death. Every member of Adam's race is savable. There is only one way of salvation. The sinner can only be justified, or declared righteous before God, through the finished work of Christ. The only way of salvation is through Christ and His finished work. His death in the stead of every man is the basis of salvation; it is the only ground upon which God can forgive sin. And what is more, only one condition of salvation is set forth in the Bible—the Lord Jesus Christ must be accepted by faith. He must be received as personal Savior; and when He is, His completed work of salvation is applied to the believer.

But what happens to all those who cannot meet this one condition of salvation? I believe firmly that all such receive eternal life. When they die, they go to Heaven. No one will spend eternity in the eternal punishment of Hell who was not able to believe, to meet God's one condition of salvation. This conviction will now be defended, first from several general Biblical considerations and then from the study of several specific passages of Scripture in the next chapter.

Dr. Lightner makes a careful and clear distinction of those who can't believe and those who refuse to believe and/or fail to respond to the revelation (in nature, in conscience, or in Scripture). Far from teaching any kind of universalism, the Scripture indicates the following:

1. All have sinned and fall short of God's glory—Romans 3:23.

2. The consequence of sin is death (separation from God)—
Romans 6:23.

3. Christ died to pay for all sin for all people of all time—
1 John 2:1–2.

4. Trusting (exercising faith) to receive God's free provision
of salvation is necessary for salvation to be appropriated
in our lives—John 1:12; Romans 5:1.

5. How does God then save and forgive those who do not
have the mental or spiritual capacity to respond? Babies,
toddlers, etc.

   a. He died for them and all mankind.

   b. Jesus demonstrated compassion for children.

   c. God's character is one of wisdom, mercy, and justice.

   d. The basis of judgment of the unsaved (Great White
   Throne) is *"judged according to what they had done
   as recorded in the books"*—Revelation 20:12.

   e. David's confidence that he would be reunited with the
   baby born of Bathsheba—2 Samuel 12:22–23.

   f. Jesus' teaching on entering the Kingdom is to become
   like a little child—Matthew 18:1–4; Mark 10:13–16.

Finally, the Scripture declares that Heaven will be populated
by people from "every nation, tribe, people and language" in

Revelation 5:9 and Revelation 7:9. It would seem logical that the death of so many who never reached the decision-making age status from the beginning of time, may be God's way of populating Heaven and fulfilling this passage.

There is hope and a certain future for those of us that have lost babies, infants, and young children who were simply unable to believe.

Hope for Hurting Parents

The following is a poem written by a young mother who lost her tiny baby to sudden infant death syndrome. Her perspective is powerful and rooted in the reality of Heaven for those who can't believe.

Two Worlds

by Rébecca Niblack at her son Lucien's funeral,

February 28, 2015

My dear little Lucien,
When you came into this world,
You discovered suffering
Amid the cries of your mother.
Your little body was crushed, stretched, contorted.
You must have wondered what was happening to you
At this inhospitable arrival,
Your sweet face bore the marks.

You left your cocoon of warmth
To discover a world of pain
And for three hours that night,
You cried, inconsolable.

You soon discovered your parents' affection
And your brothers' and sisters' excitement.
With your smiles you made them happy.
Yet, the day you were born,
You learned your first lesson:

Life on earth is filled with sorrow and misery.
For this world, once perfect,
By sin was marred,
And everywhere, like a poison, evil has infiltrated it
And brought sadness and corruption.

But in your brief human experience,
You have known neither rejection nor abandonment
    nor hatred;
You have felt neither guilt nor remorse.
You left this world without the fear or anguish of
    death . . .
Neither did you know the price paid,
To deliver you, to deliver me,
From this stain of sin.
But now you know:

I went to wake you up,
But Jesus already had.
With even more love than your mother,
He took you tenderly in his arms
To show you a different world.

Oh! I can only imagine in a very limited way
Faced with such beauty in your little astonished eyes
The splendor you have surveyed.

When I consider your two entrances into these
worlds,
What a contrast! What surprising differences . . .
If your arrival on earth was brutal and violent,
Your arrival in Heaven was nothing but love and
gentleness,
Without cries, without pain, by far the best.

And if I weep, it's not for you, oh no!
But selfishly for us who remain,
For now, in this world of sorrow,
Your absence rends our hearts.

And we mourn and we cry,
But one day we will join you
In that world
Where there is no more pain,
Nor suffering, nor tears.

2. Will there be marriage and sex in Heaven?

One day Jesus was asked a question about a woman who had been married multiple times. So the Sadducees, trying to trick Jesus, asked whom she would be married to in Heaven.

Jesus replied, *"You are in error because you do not know the Scriptures or the power of God. At the resurrection people will neither marry nor be given in marriage; they will be like the angels in Heaven"* (Matt. 22:29–30).

Jesus provides a very straightforward and clear answer to the question of marriage in Heaven. There will be no marriage in Heaven. Jesus says that we will be like the angels in that sense. He doesn't mean that we will become angels or that we are like angels in every way. He is simply saying that just as angels don't marry, we won't be married in Heaven.

Jesus doesn't elaborate on why there won't be marriage, but He is clear that there won't be marriage in Heaven. When God established marriage, it was in part because of the need Adam had for companionship. Adam was incomplete. God created marriage to give us a "taste" of belonging, love, intimacy, and connection, and He created sex for procreation, pleasure, and as a metaphor for Jesus' relationship to His church. In Heaven we won't be incomplete. We won't experience loneliness. We will experience the joy of companionship with God Himself.

God established marriage as the means of procreation and the way to fulfill God's command to be fruitful and multiply. In Heaven there will be no need for procreation.

Finally, in Heaven we will certainly have awesome and special relationships, but we won't have a need for an earthly marriage—we are part of a heavenly marriage. The Bible teaches that Christ is married to His bride, the church. In Heaven, we will experience a joy, an intimacy, a connection, and a belonging infinitely deeper than the greatest moments we've known in marriage.

As far as the question of sex, the Bible doesn't address this specifically. There will be gender in Heaven (i.e., we will maintain our maleness and femaleness) because we are made as sexual beings. But it can be inferred from Jesus' words in Matthew 22 that people won't have sexual relationships in Heaven. God gave us the gift of sex for having children, experiencing oneness, building emotional connection, and personal pleasure. These creature needs will experience deeper fulfillment in Heaven in new and infinitely better ways.

As wonderful as sex and the joy and ecstasy of being connected and in love with another human being are, Jesus has created a place and a paradigm of life that will supersede any relational or sexual experience in this life.

3. In light of Heaven, what should be our response when people die?

We all know what it is to feel the loss of someone we care about. We know what it is to stand beside a casket or sit in a funeral service and feel the pain of separation. And in that moment, it can feel so final.

In 1 Thessalonians Paul addresses how we as believers should respond to the death of other believers.

> Brothers and sisters, we do not want you to be uninformed about those who sleep in death, so that you do not grieve like the rest of mankind, who have no hope. For we believe that Jesus died and rose again, and so we believe that God will bring with Jesus those who have fallen asleep in him. (4:13–14)

Notice that Paul says we don't grieve like the rest of mankind. And the difference is the last word of verse 13. It is the word "hope." As believers, we have hope. Death is not the end. Death is not final. And while death is separation . . . for us as believers, the separation is only temporary. So while it is normal and human to feel the pain of separation and the loss of someone we love, we take tremendous comfort in knowing that the loss is temporary. And someday we will be reunited with that person.

It has always been helpful for me to see the death of believers from the perspective of Heaven. In Psalm 116:15 we read, *"Precious in the sight of the* LORD *is the death of his faithful servants."*

What we experience as loss is Heaven's gain. From God's perspective, the death of a believer is not tragic, it is not unfortunate, and it is not even sad. It is precious. Let those words sink in. The death of a believer is precious to God because it is the ultimate family reunion. It is the ultimate coming-home party.

Paul says in 1 Corinthians 15 that death has no victory over the believer. He says,

> When the perishable has been clothed with the imperishable, and the mortal with immortality, then the saying that is written will come true: "Death has been swallowed up in victory."

> "Where, O death, is your victory?
> Where, O death, is your sting?"

> The sting of death is sin, and the power of sin is the law. But thanks be to God! He gives us the victory through our Lord Jesus Christ. (vv. 54–57)

The sting of death has been overcome by the victory that is ours through Jesus Christ.

4. What about hell?

As wonderful and awesome as Heaven will be, the Bible does clearly teach that there is a place of judgment and torment called hell. When God created each person with a soul, He made that soul immortal and eternal. After your life on this earth, you will live somewhere for all of eternity.

Also, when God created you, He gave you a will and the freedom of choice. And God has bound Himself to honor your choice. He has never forced anyone to love Him or be in relationship with Him.

The good news is that, even though we are sinners, God sent Jesus and provided a way to Heaven. Because God is holy, He cannot ignore sin and sin cannot be allowed into Heaven. If a person rejects the provision of God and says no to Jesus, the Bible says that they will live forever separated from God in a place called hell. In John 5, Jesus says,

> Do not be amazed at this, for a time is coming when all who are in their graves will hear his voice and come out—those who have done what is good will rise to live, and those who have done what is evil will rise to be condemned. (vv. 28–29)

The Bible also teaches that our eternity is determined by this life.

In John 3:36 Jesus says, *"Whoever believes in the Son has eternal life, but whoever rejects the Son will not see life, for God's wrath remains on them."*

Our choice to accept or reject Jesus is the dividing line between an eternity in Heaven and an eternity in hell.

Hebrews 9 says that *"it is appointed unto men once to die, and after this the judgment"* (v. 27 KJV). So the decision you make about Christ in this life determines your eternal destiny. And after a person has died, their eternal destiny is set and cannot be changed.

It is uncomfortable to talk about hell. It should make us uncomfortable, because it is a terrible place of eternal judgment. But people go there not because God is capricious and arbitrary. People end up in hell because of their choice to reject Jesus. The reality of hell should motivate us to share the good news of Jesus with our friends and family and co-workers. You can confidently look people in the eye and tell them that Jesus loves them and that God wants to be with them forever in Heaven. There is no greater joy in life than to be able to help someone find eternal life in Jesus.

5. Is Jesus the only way to Heaven?

In this book I have been trying to help you have an accurate understanding of Heaven. I want you to begin to comprehend the wonderful gift that God has in store for you in Heaven. But here is the sobering irony: you could have a thoroughly Biblical understanding of Heaven and not go there.

The most important thing about Heaven is not understanding it; the most important thing about Heaven is making sure you go there. The good news is that the Bible is very clear about how we get to Heaven. Just like there is a lot of conjecture from people about what Heaven is like, there is a lot of conjecture about how people get to Heaven.

The entire basis of this book was examining what the Bible actually says about Heaven. And in the same way, it is important for us to understand what the Bible actually says about salvation and how to get to Heaven.

In Acts 4, Peter is talking about Jesus and His death on the cross when he says, *"Salvation is found in no one else, for there is no other name under Heaven given to mankind by which we must be saved"* (v. 12).

The Bible says there is no other name under Heaven except the name of Jesus where salvation can be found.

But it is not only Peter who declares this, Jesus Himself also declares the same truth. In John 14:6, *"Jesus answered, 'I am the way and the truth and the life. No one comes to the Father except through me.'"*

Jesus is the way, the truth, and the life . . . and NO ONE comes to the Father except through Him. That is not my claim for Him, that is His claim for Himself. And either He is who He claimed to be or He should be dismissed as a deranged lunatic. Jesus doesn't leave any room for another way to Heaven. He is THE way. He is not one of many ways. He is the only way.

And the good news is Jesus has already done everything needed to provide you a place in Heaven. You must simply receive the free gift of salvation. You can't earn it or be good enough to merit it. In perhaps the most famous verse in the Bible, we have an invitation from the lips of Jesus Himself. He said,

> For God so loved the world that he gave his one and only Son, that whoever believes in him shall not perish but have eternal life. (John 3:16)

I love that word "whoever." That includes me . . . and it includes YOU!

Eternal life and a place in Heaven can be yours today if you believe that Jesus is who He claimed to be. And if you would believe that He died on the cross for your sin and you choose to turn from your sin and become His follower, you can be saved. God wants a relationship with you . . . today and forever!

For an expanded explanation of how to have eternal life and know with certainty you have a place in Heaven, watch the link below. It's a message that more fully explains God's gift of salvation and how to know with certainty that you've received it.

livingontheedge.org/salvation

NOTES

1. Ron Charles, "'Boy Who Came Back from Heaven' Actually Didn't; Books Recalled," *Washington Post*, January 16, 2015, http://www.washingtonpost .com/blogs/style-blog/wp/2015/01/15/boy-who-came-back-from-Heaven-going -back-to-publisher/.

2. Ibid.

3. Judy Garland as Dorothy, *The Wizard of Oz*, directed by Victor Fleming (MGM, 1939).

4. Eric Metaxas, "Science Increasingly Makes the Case for God," *Wall Street Journal*, December 25, 2014.

5. Joseph M. Stowell, *Eternity: Reclaiming a Passion for What Endures* (Grand Rapids: Discovery House, 2006), 9.

6. Ibid., 52–53.

7. Stacy and Paula Rinehart, *Living in Light of Eternity* (Colorado Springs: Nav-Press, 1986), 15.

8. Russell Crowe as Maximus, *Gladiator*, directed by Ridley Scott (Universal City, CA: DreamWorks, 2000), DVD.

9. C. S. Lewis, *The Problem of Pain* (New York: HarperCollins, 2001), 130.

10. *Zondervan Pictorial Encyclopedia of the Bible*, vol. 3 (Grand Rapids: Zondervan, 1980), s.v. "Heavens, New (and Earth, New)."

11. C. S. Lewis, *Readings for Meditation and Reflection*, ed. Walter Hooper (New York: HarperCollins, 1992), 78.

12. C. S. Lewis, *Mere Christianity* (New York: MacMillan, 1980).

13. Ian Charleson as Eric Liddell, *Chariots of Fire*, directed by Hugh Hudson (Century City, CA: Twentieth Century Fox, 1981).

14. Helen H. Lemmel, "Turn Your Eyes upon Jesus," 1922.

15. Nelson Glueck, *Rivers in the Desert: History of Negev* (Philadelphia: Jewish Publication Society of America, 1969), 31.

16. Terry Hall, "How We Got Our Old Testament," *Moody Monthly*, January 1987, 32–34.

17. Peter W. Stoner, *Science Speaks* (Chicago: Moody Press, 1976).

18. The research, notes, and references for this appendix are a summary from the series *Why I Believe*, available on CD, DVD, and for small group study at www .livingontheedge.org.

Chip Ingram is the CEO and teaching pastor for Living on the Edge, an international teaching and discipleship ministry, and senior pastor of Venture Christian Church in Los Gatos, California. His passion is to help everyday Christians actually "live like Christians" by raising the bar of discipleship. A pastor for over twenty-five years, Chip has a unique ability to communicate truth and winsomely challenge people to live out their faith. Chip is the author of thirteen books, including *Finding God When You Need Him Most*; *True Spirituality: Becoming a Romans 12 Christian*; *Good to Great in God's Eyes*; and *God: As He Longs for You to See Him* Chip and his wife, Theresa, have four children and ten grandchildren. For more information about Chip Ingram, please visit www.LivingOnTheEdge.org.

Lance Witt is the founder of REPLENISH (www.replenish.net), a ministry dedicated to helping those in Christian leadership live and lead from a healthy soul. He is also the author of the book *Replenish*. Lance served for twenty years as a senior pastor and six years as an executive/teaching pastor for Saddleback Church. While at Saddleback, he helped lead the 40 Days of Purpose and 40 Days of Community campaigns. He has been married to his wife, Connie, for thirty-seven years, and they have two grown children and four granddaughters.

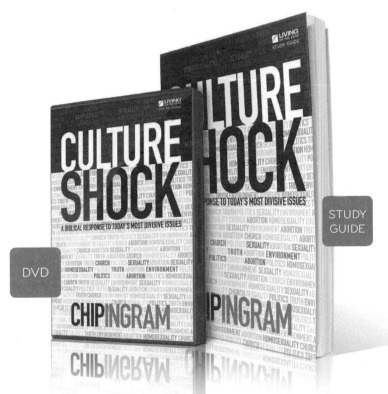

ALSO AVAILABLE

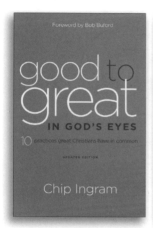

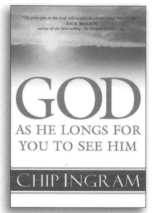

"This book will redirect, empower, and inspire you on your own journey to greatness."

—**Gregg Dedrick**, former president, KFC

The Invisible War is a balanced and Biblically informed book that examines what every believer needs to know about Satan, demons, and spiritual warfare.

God: As He Longs for You to See Him is an accessible but challenging look at the attributes of God and shows that our view of God impacts every decision in our lives.

FROM CHIP INGRAM

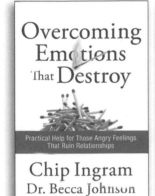

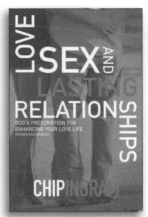

"I loved this book! From the searing first sentence, it delivers on its promise to lay bare the common failings of the human heart."

—**Gary Thomas**, author of *Sacred Marriage* and *Holy Available*

Whether single, single again, or wanting more from your marriage, you can begin the delightful journey toward a lasting, loving relationship. This practical, insightful book will show you how.

If you're fed up with our sex-saturated culture and are tired of being told to "just wait until you're married," then check out the Biblical understanding of sexuality.